D1522216

Original Title: Martial Arts Guidebook
First Edition: September 2024
First Print Run: September 2024

Website: www.sitantaichi.com

Printed in USA
Printed by Amazon Book Publishing

WUSHU GUIDEBOOK

Sitan Tai Chi & Martial Arts
www.sitantaichi.com

Contents 目录

Foreword
前言

This guidebook is based on the International Wushu Federation (IWUF)'s official, standardized routines and our experience teaching wushu to students in the United States. At the request of our students and their parents, we created this book.

I would like to thank IWUF for their videos, books, and other resources that were used to compile this guidebook. Thank you to Alan Huang and Alex Chen for their role in translating the wushu movements and proofreading the text. The terms for this information are not always easily converted between English and Chinese, so I am grateful for their help. Thank you to Scout Chen for helping to create the front and back covers, and editing the pictures. Thank you to Yan Jiang, the layout designer for this book. Most importantly, I would like to thank all students for motivating me to create this guidebook as a way to help anyone who is passionate about Wushu.

这本书是根据国际武术联合会制定的规范教程，我们多年的教学经验及在美学习武术学生的实际情况，应家长和学生的要求编写而成。

这里要特别感谢国际武术联合会为编写这本学习指南所提的技术书籍、视屏和其他资源，感谢优秀华裔武术青年Alan Huang 和 Alex Chen根据自身习练实践 帮忙翻译武术动作和校对文本。感谢Scout Chen 对封面和封底的设计及图片的修饰，感谢本书的版面设计师 Yan Jiang。最重要的是，要感谢所有的学生，他们一直激励我编写这本指南，为所有爱好和参加武术习练者提供有益的指导。

What is Sitan Tai Chi?
什么是思坦太极

Tai Chi 太极

Tai Chi originated from the ancient Chinese Taoist philosophy as a way for people to understand the world. It is a full body exercise which aims to aid in achieving a balance between the practitioner and nature, other people, and themselves.

太极来源于中国最古老的道家哲学,是人们认识世界的一种方法。太极拳是基于太极。是通过肢体带动全身心的练习来达到自身、人与人以及人与自然的平衡的运动。

Sitan Tai Chi 思坦太极

Sitan Tai Chi is a school based in New York, founded by the first champion of the World Wushu and Tai Chi Championships from China, Mr. Sitan Chen. Its mission is to promote Wushu and Tai Chi through standardized courses and qualified teachers.

思坦太极是由中国第一位世界武术锦标赛男子太极拳冠军陈思坦先生在纽约创立的太极学校,传授普及标准化武术太极套路。是运用标准化教程、合格化师资、科学化管理的太极武术学校。

Sitan Tai Chi Syllabus
思坦太极教学大纲

Syllabus Purpose 大纲目标

In addition to being created in accordance with the "Physical and Cultural Education Curriculum Guidelines"as a means of objective standardization, this syllabus adapts to the needs of modern society to study Taichi while still maintaining the characteristics of Sitan Tai Chi. It is shaped by our many years of teaching experience at home and abroad, adhering to the principle of "inheriting but not adhering to the past, developing but not forgetting the roots" and breaking the traditional pattern of learning superficial moves. We advocate for a teacher-led, student-oriented environment with the goal of achieving high quality physical education that can benefit students for the rest of their lives. The curriculum covers three practices - Tai Chi, Wushu, and Qigong - which include the pretreatment and prevention of common sports injuries and complement other aspects of traditional Chinese culture, including Chinese medicine, calligraphy, and art.

为深入进行教学探索,适应现代人对太极的需求,规范教学管理,我们根据体育文化课程指导纲要,结合思坦太极特色,编写了思坦太极教学大纲。本大纲是我们多年的海内外教学实践总结,本着"继承而不泥古,发扬而不离宗"的思想,打破只跟师傅学拳套动作的传统模式,加强全面素质教育为依据,健康第一为主导,提倡老师为主导,学生为主体,增强体质为目的,使学生终身受益。大纲中的教学内容涵盖太极、武术、健身气功三部分内容,补充太极武术与传统文化,中医、书法、艺术的结合;常见运动损伤预处理、运动性疾病预防等。

Syllabus Goals 思坦太极教学的目的任务

To understand the concept of Tai Chi and Wushu and its basic routines.
了解太极武术基本概念,掌握基本的太极武术套路。

To cultivate an active spirit; fully grasp the fundamental exercise techniques and methods.
培养体育精神,掌握正确运动技能和科学锻炼方法。

To appreciate Chinese culture through learning Tai Chi and Wushu.
通过运动进一步认识文化,运动与文化相结合。

The principle of this program: "inheriting but not adhering to the past, developing but not forgetting the roots." We provide tailor-made plans for each student depending on their current skill level that will allow them to develop their skills gradually.
大纲的选编原则:本着继承而不泥古,发扬而不离宗的原则,从学生的实际情况出发,结合当前国际上使用的教材,由浅入深,由易到难,体现其科学性和系统性。

Student, Instructor, and Staff Codes
学生，教师及工作人员守则

Student Code 学生守则

Set up personal goals and maintain a positive attitude.
明确学习目的、端正学习态度。

Show respect to all teachers, classmates, and staff.
尊重老师、同学和工作人员。

Abide by the school rules and follow the teacher's instructions.
严格遵守纪律、认真听讲,尽力完成老师的教学内容与安排的任务。

Arrive to class on time. If not able to attend class, notify the school 24 hours in advance to schedule a makeup.
准时上课,不迟到、 不早退、 不旷课,若有事须提前24小时请假,并找时间进行补课。

Respect the school's property and equipment. If there are damages made, compensation and a written apology may be required according to the circumstances.

爱护思坦太极,如损坏环境与器材将根据情节给予赔偿,并写书面检查。

Always wear the appropriate uniform and shoes in class.

上课须着思坦太极服装,鞋。

Bring all personal items with you in and out of class.

个人使用器材须装包进出学校。

Instructor Code 教师守则

Have and showcase passion for Tai Chi and Wushu. Actively participate in activities organized by Sitan Tai Chi and serve as a role model for others.

热爱太极武术教学事业,积极参加思坦太极组织的各项活动,努力把自己培养成为高素质的教学人员,以身作则、为人师表,做到教学育人。

Prepare class plans according to the Teaching Program. Once approved, any further changes should be reported to the school.

严格执行教学大纲,按教学进度编写教案,不得随意变更,若有变动须上报、批准。

Be ready 10 minutes before class begins. Instructions should be concise and to the point, while movements should be demonstrated accurately.

每次上课必须提前10分钟做好课前准备,课堂讲解简明扼要、突出重点,示范动作力求准确无误。

Enforce classroom discipline and regularly check student attendance.

严格要求学生,加强组织性、纪律性,执行考勤制度。

Frequently review and improve upon teaching material. Each instructor should host a demo class every semester, while also attending and taking notes of others' lectures.

积极开展教学科研活动,不断进行教学改革,提高业务水平和科研能力,努力提高教学效果,每位老师每学期安排一次观摩教学,参与一次其他老师的课并做好听课笔记。

Classes cannot be changed without the consent of the school. If scheduling conflicts arise, request changes in advance so that proper arrangements can be made.

未经学校同意,不得随意调课,因故不能上课须提前一天请假,以便统一安排代课事宜。

Safety first; regularly inspect the training carpet, equipment, and facilities. During class, pay attention to student behavior to avoid injury.

注意安全,认真检查场地、器材设施。注意动作、距离和练习过程的安全性。

Wear the appropriate uniform for class and maintain a serious attitude.

上课必须穿思坦太极服装,教态严谨。

Organize class schedules by semester in accordance with the syllabus.

根据大纲制定课程内容,安排每学期课程。

Cooperate with all teachers and students; prepare classrooms and other class materials.

配合老师和学生工作,准备好教学所需环境与物品。

Record student and teacher information.

做好学生和老师的资料统计。

Communicate with parents, regulatory bodies and the public.

负责教师和学员及家长的沟通与交流,加强与伙伴组织与外界的联系。

Help shape and uphold the vision of the school.

协助塑造和维护学校的愿景。

Definition, Origin and Development of Wushu
武术的定义,起源与发展

What is Wushu? 武术的定义

Fundamentally, Wushu is a Chinese martial art of combat and self defense. In practice, it takes the forms of Taolu (choreography) and Sanda (sparring) as traditional sports emphasizing the cultivation of both integrity and physique. Modern Wushu helps students understand the meaning of traditional Wushu movements while simultaneously developing their body coordination, strength, flexibility, balance, and stamina are developed through exercise of movements.

武术是以竞技动作为主要内容,以套路、散打、功法为运动形式,注重内外兼修的中国传统体育项目。现代少儿武术,主要是通过徒手和器械的练习,了解武术的攻防含义,并借助动作练习来发展少儿的协调、力量、柔韧、平衡、弹跳和耐力等基本体能和专项素质。

Origin of Wushu 武术的起源

Wushu can be traced back to ancient Chinese society, a collection of offensive and defensive techniques accumulated through field hunting experience. The martial art was used as a means of survival, but over time, it would become much more. During the Shang and Zhou dynasties, "martial dance" was used as a modified Wushu performance to train soldiers and to encourage their fighting spirits. During the Warring States period, feudal lords placed great emphasis on the physical combat skills used in the battlefield. One of these lords, Qi Huan Gong, regularly held wrestling contests in order to find exceptional soldiers to lead his armies; it was during this period that the forging of the sword and swordsmanship were unprecedentedly developed. Over the Qin and Han dynasties, grappling and fencing became popular customs in banquet parties. This swordsmanship would be showcased in many performances and stories, its style being similar to modern Wushu routines. Wushu would quickly evolve not only as a method of combat, but also as forums of recreation and physical therapy with the development of spear fighting and Hua Tuo's "Five Animals."

中国武术的起源可以追溯到原始社会。当时的人类用棍棒等工具与野兽搏斗,逐渐积累了一些攻防经验。而商代产生田猎更被视为武术训练的重要手段。商周时期,利用「武舞」来训练士兵,鼓舞士气。故认为武术可以以舞蹈形式演练。春秋战国时期,各诸侯国都很重视格斗技术在战场中的运用。齐桓公举行春秋两季的「角试」来选拔天下英雄。在这时期,剑的制造及剑道都得到了空前的发展。秦汉时期,盛行角力、击剑,有宴乐兴舞的习俗。鸿门宴中即有项庄舞剑。其形式更接近于今天武术的套路。汉代枪的应用达到颠峰,各种枪法开始出现。据传华佗首创「五禽戏」,是中国武术医疗应用的滥觞。

Tai Chi and Wushu Etiquette
太极武术礼仪

Wushu is considered one of China's national sports, as a direct method of cultivating the body and mind. It emphasizes the spirit of integrity, physique, attitude, morality, and temperament. Historically, practitioners were taught to "learn the etiquette before the art" and "understand morality before wushu." About two thousand years ago, it was recorded in the Book of Changes (Yi-jing) that "as Heaven's movement is ever changing, man must ceaselessly strive to improve." Wushu takes this philosophy and transforms it into an art which properly hones the practitioner's martial spirit.

武术是一项中国民族体育项目，更是一种最直接有效的体育与德育。武术重视对人的人格、体格、礼仪、道德、气质的教育与培养。历来强调"未曾习艺先识礼,未曾习武先明德"。早在两千多年前的《周易·象传》就提出"天行健,君子以自强不息","地势坤,君子以厚德载物",武术的"尚武与崇德"正是继承和发扬了这两种精神。

Martial honor encompasses honor of the heart, voice and body. For the heart, one must have a sense of justice and behave righteously. Always be kind, honest, respectful, and helpful. For the voice, one must not easily judge, belittle, or slander others. For the body, one must learn to respect others, to learn from their strengths to overcome one's shortcomings. Never attack with the intention to harm or take advantage of another; even during matches, have mercy and do not go any further than necessary.

武德具体还包括"心德、口德和手德"。"心德"是指为人要心存正义,讲道德。要与人为善、以诚待人,尊师重道,乐于助人等。"口德"是指无论何时何地,不要对别人妄加评论,更不能贬低别人,抬高自己；不搬弄是非。"手德"是指同道相遇,要互相学习,互相尊重,要取别人之长,补自己之短,不可存心打人、伤人,更不能乘人之危,加害别人。即使交流技艺时,也要点到为止,手下留情。

Wushu Salute: Let the left hand be a palm and the right hand be a fist. The left hand is to cover the knuckle side of the right fist. Then, form a circle in front of the chest with the arms. The left palm represents the cultures and philosophies while the right fist represents the athletic movements. To put the two together symbolizes the simultaneous cultivation of both the mind and body.

抱拳礼: 左手为掌,右手为拳,以左拳心掩右拳面,两臂环抱胸前。含义:左掌为文、右拳为武,文武兼修；左掌掩右拳表示"勇不滋事","武不犯禁"；两臂环抱表示以武会友,天下武林是一家。

Basics of Wushu
武术基本功与基本动作
Basic Movements 基本动作

Four types of straight leg kicks: Straight kick (zhèng tī tuǐ), side kick (cè tī tuǐ), outside kick (wài bǎi tuǐ), inside kick (lǐ hé tuǐ)
四种直摆性腿法:正踢腿、侧踢腿、外摆腿、里合腿

Three types of slap kicks: Slapping inside kick (jī xiǎng lǐ hé tuǐ), slapping outside kick (jī xiǎng wài bǎi tuǐ), slap kick (qián pāi jiǎo)
三种击拍性腿法:击响里合腿、击响外摆腿、前拍脚

Three types of bent leg kicks: Snap kick (tán tuǐ), heel kick (dēng tuǐ), side heel kick (cè chuài tuǐ)
三种屈伸性腿法:弹腿、蹬腿、侧踹腿

Two types of sweep kicks: Front sweep (qián sǎo), back sweep (hòu sǎo)
两种扫转性腿法:前扫、后扫

Three types of hand forms: Fist (quán), palm (zhǎng), hook (gōu)

三种手型:拳、掌、勾

Five types of stances: Front/bow stance (gōng bù), horse stance (mǎ bù), drop/crouch stance (pū bù), empty stance (xū bù), cross leg stance (xiē bù)

五种步型:弓步、马步、仆步、虚步、歇步

Five types of jumps: Front stride (dà yuè bù qián chuān), jump front kick (téng kōng fēi jiǎo), tornado kick (xuán fēng tuǐ), lotus kick (téng kōng bǎi lián), cartwheel/aerial (cè shǒu fān/kōng fān), butterfly kick (xuàn zǐ)

五种基本跳跃:腾空飞脚、旋风腿、腾空摆莲、侧手翻/空翻、旋子

Movement Requirements 动作要求

1.Hand Forms (shǒu xíng)

Fist (quán): Curl the five fingers in with the thumb over the second knuckle of the index and middle fingers. The end and top of the fist should be flat.

Palm (zhǎng): Curl in the thumb while keeping the other four fingers straight and together.

Hook (gōu): Hold the tips of the five fingers together.

手型

拳:五指卷曲,拇指扣在食指和中指的第二指节处,拳面要平。拳分为拳面、拳背、拳心、拳眼、拳轮五个部分。拳背向上为平拳。拳眼向上为立拳。

掌:拇指弯曲、其余四指伸直并拢,向后伸展。掌分为掌心、掌背、掌根。

勾:五指撮拢屈腕。勾分为勾尖、勾顶。

2.Hand Techniques (shǒu fǎ)

Punch (chōng quán): Punch quickly from the waist out, channeling all force into the front of the fist.

Drop Punch (zāi quán): Punch downward, starting with a bent arm and straightening as the punch is completed.

Hammer Fist (zá quán): Reach up with arm, then smash fist down into the other hand in front of the stomach.

Arm Chop (pī quán): Straighten arm out from up to down, hitting with the side of the fist.

Elbow Swing (pán zhǒu): Wrap the arm inwards, parallel to the floor.

Elbow Strike (dǐng zhǒu): Bend the arm and push the elbow out.

Block (gé zhǒu): Hold arm out perpendicular to the floor with fist facing upward, blocking with the forearm.

Push Palm (tuī zhǎng): Push the palm outwards from the waist, channeling all force into the "heel" of the palm.

Show Palm (liàng zhǎng): Raise the arm above the head and flick the palm inwards.

Pierce Palm (chuān zhǎng): Extend the arm out, channeling all force into the tip of the palm.

Flick Palm (tiǎo zhǎng): Flick the palm upwards through the wrist.

手法

冲拳:拳从腰间迅速向前旋臂击发,力达拳面。

栽拳:臂由曲到伸,自上向下或向前下栽出,速度要快,力达拳面。

砸拳:臂上举,然后屈臂下砸,拳心向上力达拳背。

劈拳:拳自上向下,或自后经体侧向前快速劈击,臂伸直,拳眼或拳心向上,力达拳轮。

盘肘:手臂平,拳心向下,前臂由外向内盘肘。

顶肘:屈肘握拳,拳心向下,向侧或向前顶,力达肘尖。

格肘:前臂上屈,拳心或拳眼向里,力在前臂。向内横拨为里格,向外横拨为外格。

推掌:掌从腰间迅速向前旋臂立掌推击,手臂要直,力达掌外沿。推掌也称为击掌。

亮掌:臂微屈,抖腕翻掌于体侧或头上方。

穿掌:掌心向上,臂由屈到伸,沿身体某一部位穿出,力达指尖。

挑掌:臂由下向上翘腕立掌上挑,力达四指。

3.Stances (bù xíng)

Front/Bow Stance (gōng bù): Place one leg in front of the other. Face the front foot forwards and keep both feet entirely on the floor. Bend the front leg 90 degrees and straighten the back leg.

Horse Stance (mǎ bù): Separate the legs to a little wider than the shoulders with both feet facing forwards and entirely on the ground. Bend down to where both legs are bent at 90 degrees.

Drop/Crouch Stance (pū bù): Separate the legs to twice the width of the shoulders with both feet facing forwards and entirely on the ground. Bend down towards one side so that one leg is straight while the other is bent as far as possible.

Empty Stance (xū bù): Lightly place one leg in front of the other. Bend all the way down keeping most of the weight on the back leg. The entire back foot should be on the ground but the front heel should be off the ground.

Cross-Legged Stance (xiē bù): Cross one leg over the other, then squat down to the point of sitting on the heel of the back foot, which should be off of the ground. The entire front foot as well as the tip of the back foot should still be on the ground.

Cross-Legged Sitting Stance (zuò pán): Cross one leg over the other, then sit down on the floor. The front leg should be held against the body while the back leg should be flat on the ground.

Cross-Legged Squat (chā bù): Cross one leg far behind the other. Bend down to where the front leg is bent at

90 degrees. The heel of the back foot should be off of the ground, while the entire front foot and the tip of the back foot should still be on the ground.

Toe-Pointed Step (dīng bù): Place one leg in front of the other. Bend down around halfway, with only the entire front foot and the tip of the back foot on the ground. Most of the weight should be on the front foot.

步型

弓步:前脚微内扣,全脚着地,屈膝半蹲,大腿成水平,膝部约与脚尖垂直；另一腿挺膝伸直,脚尖里扣,斜向前方,全脚着地。

马步:两脚开立,两脚间距约为本人脚长的三倍,脚尖正对前方,屈膝半蹲,大腿成水平。

虚步:后脚尖斜向前屈膝半蹲,大腿接近水平,全脚着地；前腿微屈,脚面绷平,脚尖虚点地面。

仆步:一腿全蹲,臀部接近小腿,全脚着地,膝与脚尖稍外展；另一腿平铺接近地面,全脚着地,脚尖内扣。

歇步:两腿交叉,屈膝全蹲。前脚全脚着地,脚尖外展；后脚脚跟离地,臀部紧贴后小腿。

坐盘:两腿交叉,叠腿下坐,臀部与后腿的大小腿及脚面均着地,前腿的大腿靠近胸部。

叉步:两腿交叉,前脚尖外摆45度,全脚着地,屈膝半蹲；大腿成水平；另一腿挺膝伸直,前脚掌着地,脚尖正向前方。

丁步:两腿半蹲并拢,一脚全脚着地支撑,另一脚停在支撑脚内侧相靠,脚尖点地。

4.Step Techniques(bù fǎ)

Cross Steps (chā bù): one leg steps back and crosses behind another leg

Cover Steps (gài bù): one leg steps forward and crosses in front of another

Switch Hop (huàn tiào bù): one leg is raised and the other leg pushes up when the first one comes down

步法

叉步chā bù:一脚经另一脚后横迈一步,两腿交叉。

盖步gài bù:一脚经另一脚前横迈一步,两腿交叉。

换跳步huàn tiào bù:一脚提起,另一脚蹬地起跳,随之提起脚在蹬地脚内侧下落。

5.Leg Techniques

Straight Kick (zhèng tī tuǐ): Kick forwards with the foot flexed and both legs straight. The tip of the foot should ideally reach the forehead. All kicks should have one foot completely on the ground.

Side Kick (cè tī tuǐ): Kick sideways with the foot flexed and both legs straight. The tip of the foot should ideally reach behind the head.

Outside Kick (wài bǎi tuǐ): Kick upwards with the foot flexed then outwards with the foot pointed while keeping both legs straight.

Inside Kick (lǐ hé tuǐ): Kick upwards with the foot

flexed then inwards with the foot pointed while keeping both legs straight.

Slap Kick (qián pāi jiǎo): Kick forwards with the foot pointed and both legs straight. When the foot is above the shoulder, slap the top of the foot with a free hand.

Snap Kick (tán tuǐ): Raise the knee up, then extend the leg forwards quickly with the foot pointed to kick above the waist. Channel all force into the tip of the foot.

Heel Kick (dēng tuǐ): Raise the knee up, then extend the leg forwards quickly with the foot flexed to kick above the waist. Channel all force into the heel of the foot.

Side Heel Kick (cè chuài tuǐ): Raise the knee up and open the hip, then extend the leg sideways quickly with the foot flexed to kick above shoulder level. Channel all force into the heel of the foot.

Front Sweep (qián sǎo): Start in a bow stance. Place hands in front of the straight leg while transitioning into a crouch stance on the opposite side, then use the waist and hands to push the straight leg forwards to sweep a circle.

Back Sweep (hòu sǎo): Start in a bow stance. Place hands underneath the straight leg while transitioning into a crouch stance on the same side, then use the waist and hands to push the straight leg backwards to sweep a circle.

腿法

正踢腿:支撑腿伸直,全脚着地,另一腿膝部挺直,脚尖勾起前踢,接近前额,动作要轻快有力,上身保持正直。

侧踢腿:支撑腿伸直,全脚着地脚尖外展,另一腿膝部挺直,脚尖勾起向耳侧踢起,上身保持正直。

外摆腿:支撑腿伸直,全脚着地,另一腿勾脚直腿向异侧踢起,经面前向同侧上方摆动,然后直腿落下,眼向前平视。

里合腿:支撑腿伸直,全脚着地,另一腿勾脚里扣直腿向同侧踢起,经面前向异侧上方摆动,然后直腿压脚落下,眼向前平视。

前拍脚:支撑腿伸直,另一腿脚面绷平向上踢摆,同侧手在额前迎拍脚面,击拍要准确响亮。

弹腿:支撑脚直立或稍屈,另一腿由曲到伸向前弹出,脆快有力,膝部挺直,高不过腰,脚面崩平,力达脚尖。

蹬腿:支撑腿直立或稍屈,另一腿由曲到伸猛力向前蹬出,脚尖勾起,膝部挺直,高不过胸,低不过腰,力达脚跟。

踹腿:支撑腿直立或稍屈,另一腿脚尖勾起由曲到伸向身体一侧猛力踹出,力达脚跟。侧踹时,上身倾斜,脚高过腰部。

前扫:从弓步开始,左脚尖外撇的同时,左腿屈膝大小腿折叠,左脚跟抬起,以左脚前掌碾地,右腿平铺,脚尖内扣,脚掌贴地向前扫转一周。

后扫:从弓步推掌开始,左脚尖内扣,左腿屈膝全蹲,成右仆步姿势,同时上体右转并前俯,两掌随转体在右腿内侧扶地,随着两手撑地,上体向右后拧转的力量,以左脚掌为轴,右脚贴地向后扫转一周。

6.Balances

Raised Knee Balance (tí xī píng héng): Raise one knee up in front of the body to above the waist and point the toe down. The standing leg should be straight and the entire foot should be on the ground.

Moon Watching Balance (wàng yuè píng héng): Bend one leg and raise the foot behind the body to above the waist with the toe pointed. The standing leg should be straight and the entire foot should be on the ground. The head should look in the same direction as the standing leg.

平衡

提膝平衡:支撑腿直里站稳,上体正直,另一腿在体前高提近胸,小腿斜垂里扣,脚面绷平内收。

望月平衡:支撑腿伸直或稍屈站稳,上体侧倾拧腰,向支撑腿同侧方上方,挺胸塌腰,另一腿在身后在支撑腿的同侧方上举,小腿屈收,脚面绷平,脚底朝上。

7.Jumping Techniques

Front Stride (dà yuè bù qián chuān): Take a big leap forward off of one foot onto the other, maintaining a straight body throughout.

Jump Snap Kick (téng kōng jiàn tán): Jump off of one leg, then snap kick the same leg in the air.

Jump Front Kick (téng kōng fēi jiǎo):

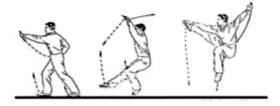

Tornado Kick (xuán fēng tuǐ):

Lotus Kick (téng kōng bǎi lián):

Cartwheel/Aerial (cè shǒu fān/kōng fān):

Butterfly Kick (xuàn zǐ):

跳跃

大跃步前穿:一脚蹬地起跳,另一脚向前跃步,前跃距离,须大于弓步,在空中挺胸抬头,肢体伸展。

腾空箭弹:身体腾空,起跳腿由屈到伸,向前蹬出,高于腰,脚面绷平,力达脚尖。

腾空飞脚:摆动腿高提,起跳腿上摆伸直,脚面绷平,脚高过肩,击打与拍脚连续快速准确响亮。

旋风腿:右脚向左前方跨一步,身体向左旋转180°,同时提起左脚顺势旋转。左脚快落地时,右脚蹬地起跳,在空中完成用右脚横踢击打左手。

腾空摆莲:腾空摆莲武术旋体跳跃动作之一,亦为腾空腿法。又名飞三响。右脚上步,脚尖稍外展,身体微右倾,左脚里合摆动,右脚随之蹬地摆起,在空中做外摆腿动作,脚面崩平,上身随之向右拧转。同时两手在头上击响(右手背击左手掌)后,再迅速分别从右向左弧形回摆,依次拍击外摆腿之脚面。

侧手翻／空翻:左脚向前迈出一步,双手依次从上往下再向前按地,要注意双手和左脚尽量保持在一条线上,右腿随即用力甩过去,仰头看地面直到翻过去,两脚落地靠近手。

旋子:开步站立,身体右转,左脚离地,左臂前平举,右臂后下举;然后左脚踏地,身体平俯向左甩动,同时两臂伸直随身向左摆动,紧接着右脚蹬地,身体悬空,两脚随身向左平旋;然后右脚先落地,左脚随之落地。

Level 1/2 Barehand Forms
初级一段拳，初级二段拳

Level 1 Barehand forms (chū jí yī duàn quán)
初级一段拳

1.并步抱拳 bìng bù bào quán
hold fists with feet together

2.马步双推掌 mǎ bù shuāng tuī zhǎng
horse stance and push both palms

3.马步格挡 mǎ bù gé dǎng
horse stance block

4.弓步冲拳 gōng bù chōng quán
bowstance punch

5.弹腿冲拳 dàn tuǐ chōng quán
punch kick with toes

6.弓步冲拳 gōng bù chōng quán
bowstance punch

7.并步砸拳 bìng bù zá quán
smash fist with feet together

8.马步架掌冲拳 mǎ bù jià zhǎng chōng quánhorse
stance with upper block and punch

9.马步抱拳 mǎ bù bào quán
horse stance hold fists on waist

10.弓步推掌 gōng bù tuī zhǎng
bowstance push palm

11.跪步抄拳 guì bù chāo quán
uppercut in kneeling stance

12.左侧摔 zuǒ cè shuāi
leg sweep onto left side

13.剪腿侧踹 jiǎn tuǐ cè chuài
scissor kick and side kick

14.乌龙绞柱 wū lóng jiǎo zhù
twist legs like dragon

15.跪步虎爪 guì bù hǔ zhǎo
tiger claw push in kneeling stance

16.并步抱拳 bìng bù bào quán
close feet and hold fists

Level 2 Barehand forms (chū jí èr duàn quán)
初级二段拳

1.并步抱拳 bìng bù bào quán
close feet and hold fists

2.马步双推掌 mǎ bù shuāng tuī zhǎng
horse stance and push both palms

3.马步格挡 mǎ bù gé dǎng
horse stance block

4.弓步冲拳 gōng bù chōng quán
bowstance punch

5.弹腿冲拳 dàn tuǐ chōng quán
punch kick with toes

6.弓步冲拳 gōng bù chōng quán
bowstance punch

7.并步砸拳 bìng bù zá quán
smash fist with feet together

8.马步架掌冲拳 mǎ bù jià zhǎng chōng quán horse
stance with upper block and punch

9.马步抱拳 mǎ bù bào quán
horse stance hold fists

10.弓步推掌 gōng bù tuī zhǎng
bowstance push palm

11.跪步抄拳 guì bù chāo quán
uppercut in kneeling stance

12.左侧摔 zuǒ cè shuāi
leg sweet onto left side

13.剪腿侧踹 jiǎn tuǐ cè chuài
scissor kick and side kick

14.乌龙绞柱 wū lóng jiǎo zhù
twist legs like dragon

15.跪步虎爪 guì bù hǔ zhǎo
tiger claw push in kneeling stance

16.并步抱拳 bìng bù bào quán
close feet and hold fists

17.开立推掌 kāi lì tuī zhǎng
open step and push palms outward

18.翻腰坐盘 fān yāo zuò pán
rotate around the waist into crossed leg sit

19.上步拍脚 shàng bù pāi jiǎo
front step slap kick

20.弓步顶肘 gōng bù dǐng zhǒu
bowstance elbow

21.仆步切掌 gōng bù qiē zhǎng
crouch stance chop

22.并步砸拳 bìng bù zá quán
smash fist with feet together

23.提膝勾手亮掌 tí xī gōu shǒu liàng zhǎng   raise
knee with upper block and hook

24.大跃步前穿 dà yuè bù qián chuān
leap forward with a long step

25.弓步冲拳 gōng bù chōng quán
bowstance punch

26.连环冲拳 lián huán chōng quán
consecutive punches

27.转身冲拳 zhuǎn shēn chōng quán
turn body and punch

28.弓步贯拳 gōng bù guàn quán
bowstance swing fist

29.并步抱拳 bìng bù bào quán
feet together and hold fists

30.直立还原 zhí lì hái yuán
closing form

C Group Changquan (Barehand) Form
初级三路拳

Characteristics of C Group Changquan 三路长拳特点

C Group Changquan consists of four sections, with a total of 36 movements. It includes three types of hand forms: fist, palm, and hook, seven types of stances: bow stance, horse stance, crouch stance, empty stance, and rest stance, thirteen types of hand techniques such as punching, chopping, piercing palm, lifting palm, elbow hitting, and elbow choking, as well as four types of leg techniques, two types of jumps, one type of balance, and various footwork.

初级三路长拳由四段组成,共36个动作,其内容包括了拳、掌、勾三种手型,弓步、马步、仆步、虚步和歇步等七种步型,冲拳、劈拳、穿掌、挑掌、顶肘、盘肘等十三种手法以及四种腿法、两种跳跃、一种平衡和各种步法。长拳的技法特点是:手要捷快,眼要敏锐、身要灵活、步要稳固、精要充沛、气要下沉、力要顺达、功要纯青,四击合法、以形喻势。

预备动作　Preparation stance

1.虚步亮掌 xū bù liàng zhǎng
empty stance with palm and hook

2.并步对拳 bìng bù duì quán
close feet and drag fists downward

第一段　　　　　　　　　Part 1

1.弓步冲拳 gōng bù chōng quán
bowstance punch

2.弹腿冲拳 dàn tuǐ chōng quán
punch kick with toes

3.马步冲拳 mǎ bù chōng quán
horse stance punch

4.弓步冲拳 gōng bù chōng quán
bowstance punch

5.弹腿冲拳 tán tuǐ chōng quán
punch kick with toes

6.大跃步前穿 dà yuè bù qián chuān
leap forward with a large step

7.弓步击掌 gōng bù jī zhǎng
bowstance push palm and hook back

8.马步架掌 mǎ bù jià zhǎng
horse stance with upper block

第二段   **Part 2**

9.虚步栽拳 xū bù zāi quán
empty stance with upper and lower blocks

10.提膝穿掌 tí xī chuān zhǎng
raise leg with left block and right palm pierce

11.仆步穿掌 pú bù chuān zhǎng
crouch stance and pierce palms

12.虚步挑掌 xū bù tiāo zhǎng
empty stance and flick palms

13.马步击掌 mǎ bù jī zhǎng
horse stance push

14.叉步双摆掌 chā bù shuāng bǎi zhǎng
cross legs and circle block with arms

15.弓步击掌 gōng bù jī zhǎng
bowstance push palm and hook back

16.转身踢腿马步盘肘
zhuǎn shēn tī tuǐ mǎ bù pán zhǒu
turn with straight kick and horsestance elbow block

第三段   **Part 3**

17.歇步抡砸拳 xiē bù lún zá quán
crossed leg stance and circle fists into smash

18.仆步亮掌 pú bù liàng zhǎng
crouch stance with palm and hook

19.弓步劈拳 gōng bù pī quán
bowstance and chop with fist

20.换跳步弓步冲拳 huàn tiào bù gōng bù chōng quán
cirlce block, twist and stomp block, and bowstance
punch

21.马步冲拳 mǎ bù chōng quán
horse stance punch

22.弓步下冲拳 gōng bù xià chōng quán
bowstance punch downward

23.叉步亮掌侧踹腿 chā bù liàng zhǎng cè chuài tuǐ
cross legs and side kick with palm and hook

24.虚步挑拳 xū bù tiāo quán
empty stance and upper fist flip

第四段   **Part 4**
25.弓步顶肘 gōng bù dǐng zhǒu
bowstance and hit with elbow

26.转身左拍脚 zhuǎn shēn zuǒ pāi jiǎo
turn and left front slap kick

27.右拍脚 yòu pāi jiǎo
right front slap kick

28.腾空飞脚 téng kōng fēi jiǎo
jump front slap kick

29.歇步下冲拳 xiē bù xià chōng quán
cross leg stance and punch

30.仆步抡劈拳 pú bù lún pī quán
circle fists and chop down into crouch stance

31.提膝挑掌 tí xī tiāo zhǎng
swing palms and raise knee

32提膝劈掌，弓步冲拳
tí xī pī zhǎng ,gōng bù chōng quán
palm chop with raised knee, bowstance punch

结束动作 Closing Form
1.虚步亮掌 xū bù liàng zhǎng
empty stance with palm and hook

2.并步对拳 bìng bù duì quán
close feet and drag fists downward

直立还原zhí lì huán yuán
Closing stance

C Group Jianshu (Straightsword) Form 初级剑术

Features of the C Group Jianshu (Straightsword):

The set of the C group Jianshu consists of four sections, with 34 movements, including preparatory and finishing moves. Its content includes seven types of footwork such as bow step, crouch step, empty step, rest step, and sitting step, as well as 14 types of sword techniques like thrusting, chopping, lifting, hanging, slashing, and pointing, along with two types of balance and various footwork.

初级剑特点:初级剑术全套共四段,34个动作,包括预备式和结束动作。其内容包括了弓步、仆步、虚步、歇步、坐盘等7种步型,刺剑、劈剑、撩剑、挂剑、斩剑、点剑等14种剑法及两种平衡和各种步法。剑术的技法特点是:轻快敏捷,身活腕灵,刚柔兼备,气韵洒脱。

剑的组成部分:

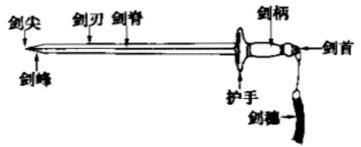

(剑尖:sword point；剑锋:sword tip；剑刃:sword
blade；剑脊:sword spine；护手:hand guand；剑
柄:sword handle；剑首:sword pommel；剑穗:sword
tassel)

主要剑法:

刺剑 cì jiàn:右手握剑,平剑或立剑向前刺出,臂与剑成
一直线,力达剑尖。
Sword thrust:arm and sword aligned, energy focused on
the sword point

劈剑 pī jiàn:右手握剑,立剑由上向下为劈,臂与剑成一
直线,力达剑身,剑刃一侧。
Sword chop:arm and sword aligned, energy focused on
one side of the sword blade

撩剑 liāo jiàn:右手握剑,立剑由下向前上方为撩,力达
剑身前部。
Circular sword cut: circle the sword from bottom to
top, bend wrist, energy focused on the front half of one
side of the sword blade

挂剑 guà jiàn:右手握剑,立剑,剑尖由前向上向后或向
下向后为挂,力达剑身前部。
Hook sword: circle the sword, let the sword point lead
the sword's path

点剑 diǎn jiàn:右手握剑,立剑提腕,使剑尖猛向下为点,力达剑尖,臂伸直。
Point sword: bend wrist downward and point the sword, energy and power at the sword point

抹剑 mǒ jiàn:右手握剑,平剑由前向左或右弧形抽回,或由后向前平带为抹,与胸或胸腹间同高,力达剑身。
Sword slide: slide the sword horizontally in a crescent between the chest and lower abdomen, energy on the sliding motion of the blade

斩剑 zhǎn jiàn:右手握剑,平剑向左或右横出为斩,力达剑身,臂伸直。
Outer sword slice: arm and sword aligned, energy and power on the outer edge of the sword blade, palm face up

截剑 jié jiàn:右手握剑,平剑,剑身斜向上或斜向下为截,力达剑身前部,臂与剑成一直线。
Diagonal sword chop: arm and sword aligned, chop the sword diagonally up or down, energy on the outer edge of the sword blade

崩剑 bēng jiàn:右手握剑,立剑沉腕,使剑猛向前上为崩,力达剑尖,臂伸直,剑尖高不过头。
Flick sword: sink the wrist and quickly flick the sword upward, energy on the sword point, sword point must be below head level

云剑 yún jiàn :右手握剑,平剑,在头顶或头前上方平圆绕环为云,仰头,以腕为轴。
Upper sword circle: use the wrist to rotate the sword above head level, look upward at the sword

剑指 jiàn zhǐ:
中指与食指伸直并拢,其余三指屈于手心,拇指压在无名指和小指的第一指节处。

Sword finger: Middle and pointer fingers must be straight and close together, bend the other three fingers, using the thumb to cover the nails of the ring and pinky fingers.

The Movements of C Group Straightsword
初级剑动作名称

预备式   Preparation Forms
并步右前指 bìng bù yòu qián zhǐclose feet and point with right sword finger

并步左前指 bìng bù zuǒ qián zhǐclose feet and point with left sword finger

虚步抱剑 xū bù bào jiàn
empty stance and grab sword at chest level

第一段   Part 1
1.弓步直刺 gōng bù zhí cì
bowstance and thrust sword forward

2.回身后劈 huí shēn hòu pī
chop sword backwards

3.弓步平抹 gōng bù píng mǒ
flat slide sword into bowstance

4.弓步左撩 gōng bù zuǒ liāo
Diagonally chop sword downward into bowstance

5.提膝平斩 tí xī píng zhǎn
circle sword upward to horizontal chop and raise knee

6.回身下刺 huí shēn xià cì
turn backward and stab downward

41

7.挂剑直刺 guà jiàn zhí cì
hook sword turn into bowstance sword thrust

8.虚步架剑 xū bù jià jiàn
empty stance with sword upper block

第二段　　　　　　　**Part 2**
9.虚步平劈 xū bù píng pī
empty stance and chop sword at should level

10.弓步下劈 gōng bù xià pī
bowstance with sword chop diagonally downward

11.带剑前点 dài jiàn qián diǎn
block sword back and point sword with forward T-step

12.提膝下截 tí xī xià jié
raise knee and chop sword diagonally downward

13.提膝直刺 tí xī zhí cì
raise knee and stab straight forward

14.回身平崩 huí shēn píng bēng
turn and horizontally chop sword with palm up

15.歇步下劈 xiē bù xià pī
downward chop into cross leg stance

16.提膝下点 tí xī xià diǎn
raise knee and point sword downward

第三段　　　　　　　**Part 3**
17.并步直刺 bìng bù zhí cì
close feet and stab forward

18.弓步上挑 gōng bù shàng tiāo
bowstance and swing sword upward

19.歇步下劈 xiē bù xià pī
downward chop into cross leg stance

20.右截腕 yòu jié wàn
small right wrist chop

21.左截腕 zuǒ jié wàn
small left wrist chop

22.跃步上挑 yuè bù shàng tiāo
leap forward into balance and flip sword upward

23.仆步下压 pū bù xià yā
crouch stance and sword blade press down

24.提膝直刺 tí xī zhí cì
raise knee and stab straight forward

第四段   **Part 4**
25.弓步平劈 gōng bù píng pī
bowstance chop at shoulder level

26.回身后撩 huí shēn hòu liāo
circular sword cut backward

27.歇步上崩 xiē bù shàng bēng
flick sword upward into cross leg stance

28.弓步斜削 gōng bù xié xiāo
diagonal outer sword slice into bowstance

29.进步左撩 jìn bù zuǒ liāo
step forward and circular sword cut on left side

30.进步右撩 jìn bù yòu liā
step forward and circular sword cut on right side

31.坐盘反撩 zuò pán fǎn liāo
circular sword cut backward into cross leg sit

32.转身云剑 zhuǎn shēn yún jiàn
turn around with upper sword circle

收势   **Closing Form**
虚步背剑,并步直立 xū bù bèi jiàn , bìng bù zhí lì
empty stance and hold sword in left hand, closing
stance

C Group Gunshu (Staff) Form
初级棍术

Features of the C group Gunshu (Staff) :

The beginner's staff technique consists of four sections with a total of 34 movements, including preparatory and closing positions. It encompasses five types of footwork: bow stance, horse stance, crounch stance, empty stance, and rest stance. It also includes 14 types of staff techniques such as chopping, deflecting, lifting, swinging, throwing, and thrusting, as well as balance, leg techniques, and various footwork.

初级棍特点:初级棍术,整套动作共四段,34个动作,包括预备式和还原势。其内容包括了弓步、马步、仆步、虚步、歇步等5种步型,劈棍、拨棍、撩棍、抢棍、摔棍、戳棍等14种棍法,及平衡、腿法和各种步法。棍术的技法特点是:换把变招,固把击发;兼枪带棒,梢把并用;棍如旋风,纵横打一片;把法多变,长短兼施.

劈棍 pī gùn：双手握棍,棍由上向下劈出,迅猛有力,力达棍前端。
Staff chop: arm and staff aligned, energy focused on the front of the staff

撩棍 liáo gùn：双手握棍,棍沿身体左侧或右侧,划立圆向前或向后撩出,速度要快,力达棍前端。
Circular staff block: circle the staff from bottom to top, energy focused front of the staff

拨棍 bō gùn：双手握棍,棍梢或棍把斜向前上方左右拨动,用力轻快平稳,幅度不要太大。
Upper staff circle: circle staff to block, look at staff

抡棍 lūn gùn：双手握棍,棍梢在胸部以上,向左或向右平抡半周以上。要求迅猛有力,力达棍前端。
Horizontal staff swing: staff must be above chest level, rotate body

摔棍 shuāi gùn：双手握棍,棍身平摔落地。要求快速有力。
Smash staff: quickly bring the staff downard and parallel to the ground with power

崩棍 bēng gùn：双手握棍,棍梢向上或向左右短促用力,力达棍梢。
Upper flip with staff head: staff point upward, energy on the front of the staff

戳棍 chuō gùn：双手握棍,棍梢或棍把直线向前、向侧或向后戳击,力达棍顶端。
Staff thrust: stab the staff with the front or base of the staff, use both hands

点棍 diǎn gùn:双手握棍,棍梢向下短促用力,力达棍梢。
Point staff: point the staff downward, bend wrist, energy on the front of the staff

挑把棍 tiāo bǎ gùn:双手握棍,棍把由下向上挑起,力达把端。
Upper flip with staff base: staff base point upward, energy on the base of the staff

C Group Gunshu (Staff) form movements
初级棍术动作名称

预备式   **Preparation stance**
并步直立 bìng bù zhí lì
Opening stance

第一段   **Part 1**
1.弓步劈棍 gōng bù pī gùn
bowstance and chop staff

2.弓步撩棍 gōng bù liāo gùn
bowstance and circular staff block forward

3.虚步上拨棍 xū bù shàng bō gùn
empty stance with circle staff above head and use front of staff to block

4.虚步把拨棍 xū bù bǎ bō gùn
empty stance with circle staff above head and use base of staff to block

5.插步抡劈棍 chā bù lūn pī gùn
cross leg step and circle staff into chap

6.翻身抡劈棍 fān shēn lūn pī gùn
turn and circle staff into horse stance chop

7.马步平抡棍 mǎ bù píng lūn gùn
horizontally swing staff and turn into horse stance

8.跳步半抡劈棍 tiào bù bàn lūn pī gùn
jump and turn into horse stance with staff chop

第二段   Part 2
9.单手抡劈棍 dān shǒu lūn pī gùn
circle staff with right hand into horstance chop

10.提膝把劈棍 tí xī bǎ pī gùn
raise knee and chop with base of staff

11.弓步抡劈棍 gōng bù lūn pī gùn
circle staff into bowstance chop

12.弓步背棍 gōng bù bèi gùn
circle staff to bowstance push with staff on back

13.挑把棍 tiāo bǎ gùn
upper flip with staff base into bowstance

14.转身弓步戳棍 zhuǎn shēn gōng bù chuō gùn
turn into bowstance and thrust staff with both hands

15.踢腿撩棍 tī tuǐ liāo gùn
spin staff and side kick

16.弓步拉棍 gōng bù lā gùn
pull the staff and downward block into bowstance

第三段   Part 3
17.提膝拦棍 tí xī lán gùn
raise knee and block sideways with staff

18.插步抡把劈棍 chā bù lūn bǎ pī gùn
cross leg step and circle staff into downward chop

19.马步抡劈棍 mǎ bù lūn pī gùn
circle block into horse stance chop

20.翻身马步抡劈棍 fān shēn mǎ bù lūn pī gùn
jump turn into horsestance chop

21.上步右撩棍 shàng bù yòu liāo gùn
step forward with right circular staff block

22.上步左撩棍 shàng bù zuǒ liāo gùn
step forward with left circular staff block

23.转身仆步摔棍 zhuǎn shēn pū bù shuāi gùn
turn into crouch stance and smash staff

24.弓步崩棍 gōng bù bēng gùn
bowstance and flip staff head upward

第四段   **Part 4**
25.马步把劈棍 mǎ bù bǎ pī gùn
forward step into horsestance and chop with staff base

26.歇步半抡劈棍 xiē bù bàn lūn pī gùn
turn into cross leg stance and chop with staff head

27.左平舞花棍 zuǒ píng wǔ huā gùn
circle staff into left bowstance with left block using
staff head

28.右平舞花棍 yòu píng wǔ huā gùn
circle staff into right bowstance with right block
using staff base

29.插步下点棍 chā bù xià diǎn gùn
cross leg step and point staff downward to the right

30.弓步下点棍 gōng bù xià diǎn gùn
bowstance and point staff donward to the left

31.插步下戳棍 chā bù xià chuō gùn
cross leg step and thrust downward with staff base

32.提膝拦棍 tí xī lán gùn
raise knee and side block with staff

结束动作   Closing Form
并步还原 bìng bù huán yuan
closing stance

C Group Daoshu (Broadsword) Form
初级刀术

Features of C Group Daoshu (Broadsword) :

Broadsword is a type of short weapon in martial arts. The practice routine of broadsword involves various techniques such as wrapping around the head, chopping, slashing, lifting, hanging, stabbing, and the coordination with the other hand, as well as various footwork and jumping movements.

刀术特点：刀术是武术器械中短兵器的一种，单刀以缠头裹脑、劈、砍、撩、挂、扎等刀法和另一手的协调配合及各种步法、跳跃动作等组成的套路练习。练起刀来，可呈现出勇猛彪悍、雄壮有力的形象，故有"刀如猛虎"的说法。

Each part of the Broadsword 刀的部位名称:

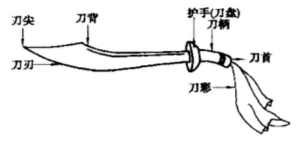

(刀尖: broadsword point; 刀刃: broadsword blade;
刀背: inner edge of broadsword; 护手: hand guard;
刀柄: broadsword handle; 刀首: broadsword pommel;
刀彩: broadsword cloth)

Basic technique of the C Group Daoshu (Broadsword)
初级刀的基本刀法:

缠头刀 chán tóu dāo
Twine broadsword around head from front

裹脑刀 guǒ nǎo dāo
Wrap broadsword around head from back

劈刀 pī dāo
Chop broadsword: arm and broadsword in line, energy
on the front of the broadsword blade

砍刀 kǎn dāo
Hack broadword: energy on the back half of the broadsword blade

撩刀 liāo dāo
Circular broadsword block

挂刀 guà dāo
Hook broadsword

扎刀 zā dāo
Thrust broadsword

藏刀 cáng dāo
Hide broadsword

扫刀 sǎo dāo
Sweep broadsword

C Group Daoshu (Broadsword) Form Movements
初级刀术动作名称

第一段   **Part 1**

1.起式 qǐ shì
Opening form

2.虚步亮掌 xū bù liàng zhǎng
hold broadsword with palm block upward in empty
stance

3.并步接刀 bìng bù jiē dāo
hold broadsword above head with feet together

4.弓步缠头 gōng bù chán tóu
twine broadsword from the front into bowstance

5.虚步藏刀 xū bù cáng dāo
empty stance and hide broadsword on right side

6.弓步前刺 gōng bù qián cì
thrust broadsword forward into bowstance

7.并步上挑 bìng bù shàng tiāo
flick broadsword upward and feet together

8.左抡劈 zuǒ lūn pī
Left circle into bowstance chop

9.右抡劈 yòu lūn pī
Right circle into bowstance chop

10.弓步撩刀 gōng bù liāo dāo
circle broadsword into bowstance block

11.弓步藏刀 gōng bù cáng dāo
bowstance and hide broadsword

第二段   **Part 2**
12.提膝缠头 tí xī chán tóu
twine broadsword from front and raise knee

13.弓步平斩 gōng bù píng zhǎn
bowstance and horizontal chop

14.仆步带刀 pū bù dài dāo
pull broadsword back into crouch stance

15.歇步下砍 xiē bù xià kǎn
 cross leg stance and broadsword hack

16.左劈刀(左转身 zuǒ pī dāo (zuǒ zhuǎn shēn)
turn around into left broadsword chop

17.右劈刀 yòu pī dāo
right broadsword chop

18.歇步按刀 xiē bù àn dāo
cross leg stance and press broadsword downward

19.马步平劈 mǎ bù píng pī
horsestance chop

第三段　　　　　Part 3

20.弓步撩刀 gōng bù liāo dāo
circular broadsword block into bowstance

21.插步反撩 chā bù fǎn liāo
cross legs and circle broadsword backward

22.转身挂劈 zhuǎn shēn guà pī
turn and hook broadsword into chop with raised knee

23.仆步下砍 pū bù xià kǎn
crouch stance and hack broadsword

24.架刀前刺 jià dāo qián cì
upper block and turn into bowstance thrust

25.左斜劈 zuǒ xié pī
left diagonal chop

26.右斜劈 yòu xié pī
right diagonal chop

27.虚步藏刀 xū bù cáng dāo
empty stance and hide broadsword

第四段　　　　　Part 4

28.旋转扫刀 xuán zhuǎn sǎo dāo
turn around and broadsword sweep

29.翻身劈刀 fān shēn pī dāo
turning jump into crouchstance chop

30.缠头箭踢 chán tóu jiàn tī
twine broadsword from front and kick with toes

31.仆步按刀 pū bù àn dāo
crouch stance and press broadsword down

32.缠头蹬脚 chán tóu dēng jiǎo
twine broadsword from front and kick with heel

33.虚步藏刀 xū bù cáng dāo
empty stance and hide broadsword

34.弓步缠头 gōng bù chán tóu
twine broadsword from front into bowstance

35.并步扫刀 bìng bù sǎo dāo
sweep broadsword and close feet together

36.接刀按掌 jiē dāo àn zhǎng
grab broadsword and palm press down

37.收式 shōu shì
closing form

C Group Qiangshu (Spear) Form
初级枪术

Features of the Spear 枪术技法特点:

The spear is the king of all weapons, characterized by its technique: the spear thrusts in a straight line, and the key to wielding it is maintaining balance in four aspects - the tip of the spear, the spear itself, the shoulder, and the foot. The front hand guides like a pipe, the back hand locks like a latch, providing stability without rigidity, and flexibility without slipping.

枪为百兵之王，其的技法特点是：枪扎一条线，持枪贵四平，即顶平、枪平、肩平，脚平；前手如管，后手如锁，稳而不死，活而不滑。

The basic spear routine consists of four sections and 30 movements, including preparatory actions and recovery positions. It includes seven types of steps such as bow step, horse step, servant step, and rest step, as well as eleven types of spear techniques such as blocking, grabbing, stabbing, chopping, and twirling the spear.

This routine focuses on blocking, grabbing, and stabbing techniques, combined with various steps such as inserting and jumping.

初级枪术整套动作共四段，30个动作，包括预备动作与还原势。其内容包括了弓步、马步、仆步、歇步等7种步型以及拦枪、拿枪、扎枪、劈枪、拨枪、舞花枪等11种枪法。该套路以拦拿扎枪为核心，结合插步、跳步等各种步法，充分体现了枪似游龙扎一点的基本技法。

Each Part of the Spear 枪的部位名称:

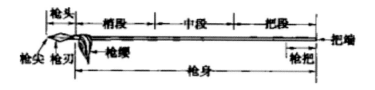

(枪尖: spear tip; 枪头: spear head; 枪缨: spear tassel; 枪身: spear shaft; 枪把: spear base

Foundation Skills of the Spear 基本枪法

Spear left circle block: both hands hold spear, spear head moves in a left circle block, spear is between head and waist
拦枪 lán qiāng: 双手握枪，枪尖向外划弧，高不过头，低不过胯。

Spear right circle block: both hands hold spear, spear head moves in a right circle block, spear is between head and waist
拿枪 ná qiāng: 双手握枪，枪尖向内划弧，高不过头，低不过胯。

Thrust spear: both hands on spear, thrust the spear forward, both hands should be together, energy at the spear tip

扎枪 zā qiāng: 双手握枪直出，劲达于枪尖，使枪颤动，后手必须触及前手。

Push spear: both hands hold spear, spear must be horizontal or vertical, push forward with both arms straight

推枪 tuī qiāng: 双手握枪呈水平或直立向体前或体侧推出，臂伸直。

Spear chop: both hands on spear, chop from up to down, energy on the spearhead

劈枪 pī qiāng: 双手握枪，由上而下劈，用力快猛，力达枪尖。

Spear sweep: both hands on spear, sweep spear left and right, lower sweeps must have the spear head between the knee and floor

拨枪 bō qiāng: 双手握枪，枪身左右拨动，用力要轻快平衡，幅度不要太大。下拨枪高不过膝，低不触地。

Spear base upper block: both hands on spear, spear base blocks from bottom to top, energy on the end of the spear base

挑把枪 tiāo bǎ qiāng: 双手握枪，枪把由下向上挑起，力达把端。

Spear downward block: both hands on spear, spear moves from the back in a forward downward motion, energy on the end of the spear base

盖把枪 gài bǎ qiāng: 双手握枪，枪把由后向前下盖，力达把端。

Circle spear block: both hands on spear, use a figure-eight shape to block on the left and right sides
舞花枪 wǔ huā qiāng： 双手握枪，枪要贴近身体，
立圆绕平，速度要快，动作要连贯。

The Movements of the C Group Qiangshu (Spear)
初级枪术动作名称

预备动作　　　　　**Preparation Movements**
虚步托枪 xū bù tuō qiāng
empty stance with spear above head

弓步扎枪 gōng bù zā qiāng
bowstance and thrust spear

第一段　　　　　**Part 1**
1.插步拦拿中平扎枪
chā bù lán ná zhōng píng zā qiāng
Cross legs and circle spear left and right into bowstance thrust

2.跳步拦拿中平扎枪
tiào bù lán ná zhōng píng zā qiāng
hop and circle spear left and right into bowstance thrust

3.绕上步拦、拿中平扎枪
rào shàng bù lán、 ná zhōng píng zā qiāng
curved step into closed feet and bowstance thrust

4.插步拦拿中平扎枪
chā bù lán ná zhōng píng zā qiāng
cross legs and circle spear left and right into bowstance thrust

第二段   Part 2

5.转身弓步中平枪
zhuǎn shēn gōng bù zhōng píng qiāng
turn around into left bowstance thrust

6.上步弓步推枪 shàng bù gōng bù tuī qiāng
step forward into bowstance and push spear

7.仆步低平枪 pū bù dī píng qiāng
crouch stance and lower thrust

8.提膝抱枪 tí xī bào qiāng
step forward into raised knee balance and hold spear

9.提膝架枪 tí xī jià qiāng
raise knee and upper block with spear

10.弓步拿、扎枪 gōng bù ná、zā qiāng
bowstance with right circle block and thrust

11.马步盖把枪 mǎ bù gài bǎ qiāng
downward block spear base into horse stance

12.舞花拿、扎枪 wǔ huā ná、 zā qiāng
figure-eight block and turn around into right circle block and bowstance thrust

第三段   Part 3

13.上步劈、扎枪 shàng bù pī、zā qiāng
step forward and chop spear into bowstance thrust

14.挑把转身拿扎枪 tiāo bǎ zhuǎn shēn ná zā qiāng
spear base upper block and turn around into bowstance thrust

15.横档步劈枪 héng dàng bù pī qiāng
side bowstance step and downward chop

16.虚步下扎枪 xū bù xià zā qiāng
empty stance and downward thrust above head

17.歇步拿枪 xiē bù ná qiāng
cross leg stance and circle right block with spear

18.马步单平枪 mǎ bù dān píng qiāng
horse stance and thrust spear with one hand

19.插步拦、拿中平扎枪
chā bù lán、 ná zhōng píng zā qiāng
cross legs and circle left and right block into
bowstance thrust

20.弓步拉枪 gōng bù lā qiāng
bowstance and pull spear

第四段　　　　　　　　Part 4
21.转身中平扎枪 zhuǎn shēn zhōng píng zā qiāng
turn around into bowstance thrust

22.转身拉枪 zhuǎn shēn lā qiāng
turn and pull spear

23.插步拔枪 chā bù bō qiāng
cross leg steps and sweep spear

24.并步下扎枪 bìng bù xià zā qiāng
close feet and thrust spear downward from head

25.跳步中平枪 tiào bù zhōng píng qiāng
hop into bowstance thrust

26.拗步盖把枪 ǎo bù gài bǎ qiāng
step forward and downward block with spear base

27.仆步劈枪 pū bù pī qiāng
circle spear and jump into crouch stance with
spear chop

28.转身弓步中平枪
zhuǎn shēn gōng bù zhōng píng qiāng
turn around into bowstance thrust

收式   **Closing Form**
虚步托枪 xū bù tuō qiāng
empty stance with spear above head

C Group Nanquan (Southern Style Barehand) Form
C 组南拳竞赛套路

第一段　　　　　　　**Part 1**

1.麒麟步弓步冲拳（发声）
qí lín bù gōng bù chōng quán (fā shēng)
Qilin step into bow stance punch (shout)

2.骑龙步推爪 qí lóng bù tuī zhǎo
dragon-riding stance and push claw

3.马步双切桥 mǎ bù shuāng qiè qiáo
horse stance and forearm chop

4.马步单指双盘桥 mǎ bù dān zhǐ shuāng pán qiáo
circle both forearms into horse stance
with pointer palm

5.马步双沉桥推指 mǎ bù shuāng chén qiáo tuī zhǐ
sink both forearms with horse stance
and push pointer palm

6.马步双标挑掌 mǎ bù shuāng biāo tiāo zhǎng
thrust palm in horse stance and bend palms up

7.右弓步双架桥 yòu gōng bù shuāng jià qiáo
block with both forearms and right bow stance

8.单蝶步右砍掌 dān dié bù yòu kǎn zhǎng
single butterfly stance and right palm chop

第二段   Part 2
9.右弓步左抛拳 yòu gōng bù zuǒ pāo quán
left fist swing upward into right bow stance

10.左弓步右抛拳 zuǒ gōng bù yòu pāo quán
right fist swing upward into left bowstance

11.左弓步推爪 zuǒ gōng bù tuī zhǎo
left bowstance and push claw

12.马步双劈拳 mǎ bù shuāng pī quán
horse stance and chop with both fists

13.右弓步双蝶掌 yòu gōng bù shuāng dié zhǎng
right bowstance and butterfly palm with both hands

14.麒麟步弓步双切掌
qí lín bù gōng bù shuāng qiē zhǎng
Qilin step into bowstance with both palms chopping

15.勒手踩腿 lè shǒu cǎi tuǐ
grab and low kick

16.弓步双切掌 gōng bù shuāng qiē zhǎng
bowstance and chop with both palms

65

第三段   Part 3

17.云手弓步推爪 yún shǒu gōng bù tuī zhǎo
circle block above head into bow stance and push claw

18.右独立步双虎爪 yòu dú lì bù shuāng hǔ zhǎo
stand on right left with both hands as tiger claws

19.左弓步挂盖 zuǒ gōng bù guà gài
left bowstance and downward swinging block hit

20.退步左右格挡 tuì bù zuǒ yòu gé dǎng
backward steps with right and left blocks

21.左弓步冲拳 zuǒ gōng bù chōng quán
left bowstance punch

22.并步抱拳 bìng bù bào quán
feet together and hold fists

23.盖步左蹬腿 gài bù zuǒ dēng tuǐ
step forward with left heel kick

24.跪步双推爪（发声）
guì bù shuāng tuī zhǎo（fā shēng）
kneeling stance and push claws
with both hands (shout)

第四段   Part 4

25.插步鞭拳 chā bù biān quán
step back and whip fist

26.转身挂盖 zhuǎn shēn guà gài
turn around and downward swinging block hit

27.跃步弓步撩爪 yuè bù gōng bù liāo zhǎo
hop into bowstance and upper circle claw

28.虚步左切桥 xū bù zuǒ qiē qiáo
empty stance and chop with left forearm

29.马步冲拳 mǎ bù chōng quán
horse stance bunch

30.弓步滚桥 gōng bù gǔn qiáo
bow stance and twist forearm block

31.弓步沉桥推指 gōng bù chén qiáo tuī zhǐ
sink forearms with bow stance and pointer palm push

32.骑龙步右担肘 qí lóng bù yòu dān zhǒu
dragon-riding stance and elbow upper hit

收势 shōu shì
closing form

C Group Nandao (Southern Style Broadsword) Form
C 组南刀竞赛套路

第一段   **Part 1**

1.左虚步盖掌 zuǒ xū bù gài zhǎng
left empty stance and push on Nandao with palm `

2.骑龙步架刀 qí lóng bù jià dāo
dragon-riding stance and upper block with Nandao

3.拐步左右下砍 guǎi bù zuǒ yòu xià kǎn
cross steps with chops on left and right sides

4.单蝶步错刀 dān dié bù cuò dāo
single butterfly stance and Nandao forward
block with palm up

5.右弓步挑刀 yòu gōng bù tiāo dāo
right bowstance and swing Nandao upward

6.独立步左右挂刀 dú lì bù zuǒ yòu guà dāo
circle block on left and right sides with knee up

7.马步格刀 mǎ bù gé dāo
horse stance and block with Nandao

8.转身右弓步截刀 zhuǎn shēn yòu gōng bù jié dāo
turn around into right bowstance and diagonally
chop downward

第二段   Part 2
9.骑龙步左平斩 qí lóng bù zuǒ píng zhǎn
dragon-riding stance and left horizontal chop

10.骑龙步右平斩 qí lóng bù yòu píng zhǎn
dragon-riding stance and right horizontal chop

11.左弓步劈刀 zuǒ gōng bù pī dāo
left bow stance with Nandao chop

12.左弓步扎刀 zuǒ gōng bù zā dāo
left bow stance with Nandao thrust

13. 丁步按刀 dīng bù àn dāo
T-step and press Nandao downward

14.跳转右弓步扎刀 tiào zhuǎn yòu gōng bù zā dāo
turn and jump into right bow stance thrust

15.独立步下砍 dú lì bù xià kǎn
stand on leg and chop downward

16.跪步立推刀 guì bù lì tuī dāo
kneeling stance and push Nandao in a vertical position

第三段   Part 3
17.麒麟步左云刀 qí lín bù zuǒ yún dāo
Qilin steps with left circle block above head

18.左弓步抹刀 zuǒ gōng bù mǒ dāo
left bow stance and slide Nandao

19.麒麟步右云刀 qí lín bù yòu yún dāo
Qilin steps with right circle block above head

20.骑龙步带刀 qí lóng bù dài dāo
dragon-riding stance and retract Nandao on right side

21.左弓步扎刀 zuǒ gōng bù zā dāo
left bow stance and Nandao thrust

22.马步截刀 mǎ bù jié dāo
horse stance and diagonally block downward

23.拐步左右扫刀 guǎi bù zuǒ yòu sǎo dāo
cross steps with Nandao sweep on left and right sides

24.半马步劈刀 bàn mǎ bù pī dāo
high horsestance with Nandao chop

第四段   **Part 4**

25.回身右弓步撩刀 huí shēn yòu gōng bù liāo dāo
turn back into right bow stance and circle uppercut

26.上步撩腕花 shàng bù liāo wàn huā
step forward and circle Nandao upward with wrist

27.麒麟步左右下砍 qí lín bù zuǒ yòu xià kǎn
Qilin steps with downward chops on left and right
sides

28.左弓步平斩 zuǒ gōng bù píng zhǎn
left bow stance and horizontally chop

29.马步挂劈刀 mǎ bù guà pī dāo
hook circle with Nandao into horse stance chop

30.跳转马步下砍 tiào zhuǎn mǎ bù xià kǎn
turn and jump into horse stance with downward chop

31.回身左弓步扎刀 huí shēn zuǒ gōng bù zā dāo
turn back into left bow stance thrust

32.半马步捧刀 bàn mǎ bù pěng dāo
high horse stance and hold broadsword

收势　shōu shì
closing form

C Group Nangun (Southern Style Staff) Form
C组南棍竞赛套路

第一段   **Part 1**

1.弓步劈棍 gōng bù pī gùn
bow stance and chop Nangun

2.马步戳棍 mǎ bù chuō gùn
horse stance and thrust Nangun

3.马步滚压棍 mǎ bù gǔn yā gùn
horse stance and rotate Nangun downward

4.插步拦拨棍 chā bù lán bō gùn
cross steps and twist staff

5.骑龙步横击把 qí lóng bù héng jī bǎ
dragon-riding stance and hit with Nangun base

6.弓步斜击棍 gōng bù xié jī gùn
bow stance and hit Nangun head diagonally upward

7.马步挑把棍 mǎ bù tiāo bǎ gùn
horse stance and upper flip with Nangun base

8.横裆步滚压棍 héng dāng bù gǔn yā gùn
sideways bow stance and press Nangun downward

第二段   **Part 2**
9.半马步挑劈棍（发声）
bàn mǎ bù tiāo pī gùn (fā shēng)
high horse stance with Nangun chop (shout)

10.右弓步云拨棍 yòu gōng bù yún bō gùn
circle block with staff above head into
right bow stance

11.左弓步云拨棍 zuǒ gōng bù yún bō gùn
 circle block with staff above head into left bow stance

12.马步挑棍 mǎ bù tiāo gùn
horse stance and flip staff upward

13.左挂棍 zuǒ guà gùn
circle hook block with Nangun on left side

14.右挂棍 yòu guà gùn
circle hook block with Nangun on right side

15.马步劈棍 mǎ bù pī gùn
horse stance and chop Nangun

16.弓步挑棍 gōng bù tiāo gùn
bow stance and flip Nangun head upward

第三段   **Part 3**
17.弓步绞戳棍 gōng bù jiǎo chuō gùn
bow stance and thrust Nangun forward

73

18.提膝拄棍 tí xī zhǔ gùn
raise knee and sideways block with Nangun

19.舞花翻跳仆步摔棍
wǔ huā fān tiào pū bù shuāi gùn
circle block on sides and jump
into a crouch stance slam

20.虚步崩棍 xū bù bēng gùn
empty stance and flip Nangun head upwards

21.弓步戳棍 gōng bù chuō gùn
bow stance and thrust Nangun forward

22.叉步下格棍 chā bù xià gé
cross steps and downward block

23.弓步戳把 gōng bù chuō bǎ
bow stance and thrust Nangun

24.舞花虚步点棍 wǔ huā xū bù diǎn gùn
circle block on sides into empty stance
and point Nangun

第四段　　　　　　　　**Part 4**
25.独立抱棍 dú lì bào gùn
stand on one leg and hold Nangun

26.虚步下拨棍 xū bù xià bō gùn
empty stance and circle Nangun downward

27.麒麟步弓步双推棍（发声）
qí lín bù gōng bù shuāng tuī gùn (fā shēng)
Qilin steps into bowstance and push Nangun
with both hands

74

28.半马步挂劈棍 bàn mǎ bù guà pī gùn
shifted horse stance and circle Nangun
downward into chop

29.骑龙步格棍 qí lóng bù gé gùn
dragon-riding stance and block with Nangun vertically

30.单蝶步摔棍 dān dié bù shuāi gùn
singly butterfly stance and slam Nangun

31.弓步劈棍 gōng bù pī gùn
bow stance and Nangun chop

32.虚步抽棍 xū bù chōu gùn
empty stance and pull Nangun backwards

收势 shōu shì
closing form

24 Form Taijiquan (Tai Chi Barehand) Form
24式太极拳

1.起势 qǐ shì
Commencing

2.左右野马分鬃 zuǒ yòu yé mǎ fēn zōng
Part the Wild Horse's Mane (left & right)

3.白鹤亮翅 bái hè liàng chì
White Crane Spreads Its Wings

4.左右搂膝拗步 zuǒ yòu Lōu xī ǎo bù
Brush Knee and Step Forward, Brush Knee and Twist
Step (left & right)

5.手挥琵琶 shǒu hūi pí pā
Playing the Lute

6.左右倒卷肱 (zuǒ yòu dào juǎn gōng)
Reverse Reeling Forearm, Step Back and Repulse
Monkey (left & right)

7.左揽雀尾 zuǒ lǎn què wěi
Left Grasp Peacock's Tail

8.右揽雀尾 yòu lǎn què wěi
Right Grasp Peacock's Tail

9.单鞭 dān biān
Single Whip

10.云手 yún shǒu
Wave Hands Like Clouds

11.单鞭 dān biān
Single Whip

12.高探马 gāo tàn mǎ
High Pat on Horse

13.右蹬脚 yòu dēng jiǎo
Kick with Right Heel

14.双峰贯耳 shuāng fēng guàn ěr
Strike to Ears with Both Fists

15.转身左蹬脚 zhuǎn shēn zuǒ dēng jiǎo
Turn Body Kick with Left Heel

16.左下势独立 zuǒ xià shì dú lì
Left Creep Down and Stand on One Leg

17.右下势独立 yòu xià shì dú lì
Right Creep Down and Stand on One Leg

18.右左玉女穿梭 yòu zuǒ yù nǚ chuān suō
Fair Lady Works with Shuttles (right & left)

19.海底针 hǎi dǐ zhēn
Needle at Sea Bottom

20.闪通臂 shǎn tōng bì
Bow stance, Pull and Push

21.转身搬拦捶 zhuǎn shēn bān lán chuí
Turn Body, Deflect, Parry, and Punch

22.如封似闭 rú fēng shì bì
Appears Closed, Withdraw and Push, as if
Closing a Door

23.十字手 shí zì shǒu
Cross Hands

24.收势 shōu shì
Closing

32 form Taijijian (Tai Chi Barehand) Form 32式太极剑

起势 qǐ shì
Commencing

第一段   Part 1

1.并步点剑 bìng bù diǎn jiàn
Feet together and point sword

2.独立反刺 dú lì fǎn cì
Stand on one leg and stab overhead

3.仆步横扫 pū bù héng sǎo
crouch stance and sweep sword

4.向右平带 xiàng yòu píng dài
bring sword to the right flat

5.向左平带 xiàng zuǒ píng dài
bring sword to the left flat

6.独立抡劈 dú lì lūn pī
circle chop on one leg

7.退步回抽 tuì bù huí chōu
step back circle withdraw

8.独立上刺 dú lì shàng cì
Stand on one leg stab up

第二段　　　　　　　**Part 2**
9.虚步下戳 xū bù xià chuō
Empty stance downwards cut

10.左弓步刺 zuǒ gōng bù cì
Left bow stance stab

11.转身斜带 zhuǎn shēn xié dài
Turn body carry across

12.缩身斜带 suō shēn xié dài
Carry across body

13.提膝捧剑 tí xī pěng jiàn
Lift knee hold sword both hands

14.跳步平刺 tiào bù píng cì
Falling step level stab

15.左虚步撩 zuǒ xū bù liāo
Left empty stance lift

16.右弓步撩 yòu gōng bù liāo
Right bow stance lift

第三段　　　　　　　**Part 3**
17.转身回抽 zhuǎn shēn huí chōu
Turn body circle withdraw

18.并步平刺 bìng bù píng cì
Feet together level stab

19.左弓步拦 zuǒ gōng bù lán
Left bow stance parry

20.右弓步拦 yòu gōng bù lán
Right bow stance parry

21.左弓步拦 zuǒ gōng bù lán
Left bow stance parry

22.進步反刺 jìn bù fǎn cì
Advance step stab overhead

23.反身回劈 fǎn shēn huí pī
Turn back circle chop

24.虚步点剑 xū bù diǎn jiàn
Empty stance point sword

第四段   **Part 4**
25.独立平托 dú lì píng tuō
stand on one leg lift hilt

26.弓步掛剑 gōng bù guà jiàn
Bow stance wheel sword back

27.虚步抡劈 xū bù lūn pī
Whirl and chop to empty stance

28.撤步反击 chè bù fǎn jī
Withdraw step and slash right

29.進步平刺 jìn bù píng cì
Step forward level stab

30.丁步回抽 dīng bù huí chōu
Fourth step circle withdraw

31.旋转平抹 xuán zhuǎn píng mǒ
Turn around level

32.弓步直刺 gōng bù zhí cì
Bow stance straight stab

收势   **Closing Form**

B Group Changquan Form
B组长拳竞赛套路

Movements of B Group Changquan
B组长拳竞赛套路动作名称

第一段   **Part 1**

1.预备式 yù bèi shì
preparation stance

2.并步按掌 bìng bù àn zhǎng
palms press down with feet together

3.并步撩掌 bìng bù liāo zhǎng
flick palms upward with feet together

4.歇步挑掌 xiē bù tiāo zhǎng
cross leg stance and flip palm

5.上步拍脚 shàng bù pāi jiǎo
step forward with front slap kick

6.弓步推掌 gōng bù tuī zhǎng
bowstance push

7.弓步刁手 gōng bù diāo shǒu
bowstance and grab into fist

8.弹踢推掌 dàn tī tuī zhǎng
push palm and kick with toes

9.左弓步冲拳 zuǒ gōng bù chōng quán
left bowstance and punch twice

10.并步砸拳 bìng bù zá quán
close feet and smash fist

11.上步拍脚 shàng bù pāi jiǎo
step forward with front slap kick

12.提膝冲拳 tí xī chōng quán
raise knee and punch

13.腾空转身摆莲 téng kōng zhuǎn shēn bǎi lián
outside lotus jump kick

14.上步弹踢 shàng bù dàn tī
step forward and punch kick with toes

15.侧身平衡 cè shēn píng héng
sideways balance with left leg back

16.并步砸拳 bìng bù zá quán
close feet and smash fist

17.马步冲拳 mǎ bù chōng quán
horse stance with both sides punch

18. 弓步推掌 gōng bù tuī zhǎng
bowstance with front and back push

19. 击响外摆腿 jī xiǎng wài bǎi tuǐ
slap outside kick

20. 高虚步劈拳 gāo xū bù pī quán
fist chop with high empty stance

21. 腾空飞脚 téng kōng fēi jiǎo
front slap jump kick

22. 提膝推掌 tí xī tuī zhǎng
raise knee and push palm

23. 上步旋风脚 shàng bù xuán fēng jiǎo
step forward into tornado jump kick

24. 马步砸拳 mǎ bù zá quán
horse stance and smash fist downward

25. 盖步双摆掌 gài bù shuāng bǎi zhǎng
cross leg step and circle both hands

26. 击步拍脚 jī bù pāi jiǎo
gallop into front slap kick

27. 仆步抡拍掌 pū bù lūn pāi zhǎng
circle arms into crouch stance downward slap

28. 抡臂砸拳 lūn bì zá quán
wheel arms and smash fist

29. 并步推掌 bìng bù tuī zhǎng
push palms outwards with feet together

30.上步正踢腿 shàng bù zhèng tī tuǐ
step forward and straight kick

31.虚步勾手 xū bù gōu shǒu
empty stance with hook

32.提膝亮掌 tí xī liàng zhǎng
raise knee with hook and palm

第二段   **Part 2**

33.仆步穿掌 pū bù chuān zhǎng
crouch stance and pierce palm

34.推掌蹬腿 tuī zhǎng dēng tuǐ
bend kick with heel and push palms outward

35.大跃步前穿 dà yuè bù qián chuān
large leap forward

36.仆步双拍掌 pū bù shuāng pāi zhǎng
crouch stance with both hands slap down

37.推掌侧踹腿 tuī zhǎng cè chuài tuǐ
bend side kick and push palms outward

38.抓肩马步架打 zhuā jiān mǎ bù jià dǎ
grab shoulder into horse stance upper block and punch

39.马步格肘 mǎ bù gé zhǒu
horse stance with elbow block

40.弓步架打 gōng bù jià dǎ
bowstance with upperblock and punch

41.横裆步亮掌 héng dāng bù liàng zhǎng
sideways bowstance with hook and palm

第三段   Part 3

42.贯拳弓步顶肘 guàn quán gōng bù dǐng zhǒu
sideways swing fist and turn into bowstance elbow hit

43.扣腿冲拳 kòu tuǐ chōng quán
pin back leg and punch

44.歇步亮掌 xiē bù liàng zhǎng
cross leg stance with hook and palm

45.插步穿抹掌 chā bù chuān mǒ zhǎng
cross leg steps with palms thrust and block

46.半马步挑掌 bàn mǎ bù tiāo zhǎng
half horse stance and flip palm

47冲拳弹腿 chōng quán dàn tuǐ
punch with feet together into push kick with toes

48.插步冲拳 chā bù chōng quán
cross legs and punch backwards

49.弧形步击响里合腿 hú xíng bù jī xiǎng lǐ hé tuǐ
crescent walk into inside slap kick

50.上步拍地 shàng bù pāi dì
step forward and slap ground

51.仆步横切掌 pū bù héng qiē zhǎng
crouch stance and horizontally chop with palm

第四段   Part 4

52.抡臂砸拳 lūn bì zá quán
wheel arms and smash fist

53.提膝抄拳 tí xī chāo quán
raise knee and upper cut fist

54.垫步旋子 diàn bù xuán zǐ
skip into butterfly jump

55.上步拍脚 shàng bù pāi jiǎo
step forward into front slap kick

56.弓步撩掌 gōng bù liāo zhǎng
bowstance and swing palms diagonally

57.弓步盘肘 gōng bù pán zhǒu
bowstance and hook with arm

58.扶地后扫腿 fú dì hòu sǎo tuǐ
backward sweep on ground

59.抡臂砸拳 lūn bì zá quán
wheel arms and smash fist

60.虚步亮掌 xū bù liàng zhǎng
empty stance and open palms

61.高虚步抱拳 gāo xū bù bào quán
high empty stance with palm and fist

62.并步直立 bìng bù zhí lì
closing stance

收势 shōu shì
closing form

B Group Jianshu (StraightSword) Form
B 组剑术竞赛套路

Movements of B Group Jianshu(Straight Sword)
B组剑术竞赛套路动作名称

第一段   **Part 1**

1.预备姿势 yù bèi zī shì
Preparation stance

2.并步亮指 bìng bù liàng zhǐ
flick sword finger with feet together

3.转身云剑 zhuǎn shēn yún jiàn
turn around with upper sword circle

4.盘腿平衡截剑 pán tuǐ píng héng jié jiàn
cross leg balance with sword chop

5.上步撩剑 shàng bù liāo jiàn
forward step and circular sword cut

6.提膝抱剑 tí xī bào jiàn
raise knee and hold sword

7.行步带剑 xíng bù dài jiàn
crescent step and hold sword

8.上步撩剑 shàng bù liāo jiàn
step forward and circular sword cut

9.扣步点剑 kòu bù diǎn jiàn
inside step and point sword downward

10.插步腕花 chā bù wàn huā
cross leg step and sword circle around wrist

11.弓步刺剑 gōng bù cì jiàn
bowstance thrust with sword

12.并步点剑 bìng bù diǎn jiàn
point sword downward with feet together

13.退步抹剑 tuì bù mǒ jiàn
step back and slide sword left and right

14.退步撩剑 tuì bù liāo jiàn
step back and upper circle cut with sword

15.跳提膝撩剑 tiào tí xī liāo jiàn
raised knee hop and upper circle cut with sword

16.上步刺剑 shàng bù cì jiàn
step forward with sword thrust

17.弓步刺剑 gōng bù cì jiàn
bowstance thrust with sword

18.并步撩剑 bìng bù liāo jiàn
close feet and circular sword cuts

19.虚步刺剑 xū bù cì jiàn
empty stance and thrust sword

20.并步截剑 bìng bù jié jiàn
diagonal sword chop downward with feet together

21.上步挂剑 shàng bù guà jiàn
step forward with hook sword left and right

22.翻身抡挂剑 fān shēn lūn guà jiàn
rotate body with hook sword

23.退步挂剑 tuì bù guà jiàn
step back with hook sword left and right

24.插步撩剑 chā bù liāo jiàn
cross legs and circular sword cut upward

25.并步劈剑 bìng bù pī jiàn
close feet and chop sword backward

26.行步带剑 xíng bù dài jiàn
crescent steps and hold sword

27.歇步抱剑 xiē bù bào jiàn
 cross leg stance and hold sword

28.转身云剑 zhuǎn shēn yún jiàn
turn around and sword circle above head

29.仆步穿剑 pū bù chuān jiàn
crouch stance and pierce sword

30.弓步压剑 gōng bù yā jiàn
bowstance and press sword down

31.退步绞剑 tuì bù jiǎo jiàn
step back and spin sword point

32.坐盘崩剑 zuò pán bēng jiàn
cross leg sit and flick sword

33.望月平衡撩剑 wàng yuè píng héng liāo jiàn
crescent back balance with upper circle cut

第三段   Part 3
34.插步撩剑 chā bù liāo jiàn
cross legs and circle sword cut backwards

35.上步刺剑 shàng bù cì jiàn
step forward and thrust sword

36.换跳步刺剑 huàn tiào bù cì jiàn
switch leg hop and thrust sword

37.翻腰扫剑 fān yāo sǎo jiàn
rotate around waist and sweep sword

38.转身扫剑 zhuǎn shēn sǎo jiàn
turn around and sweep sword

39.退步腕花 tuì bù wàn huā
step back and sword circle around wrist

40.翻腰抡劈剑 fān yāo lūn pī jiàn
rotate around waist and sword circle into chop

41.弓步崩剑 gōng bù bēng jiàn
bowstance and flick sword

42. 击步点剑 jī bù diǎn jiàn
gallop and point sword downward

43. 翻身挂剑 fān shēn guà jiàn
rotate body vertically and hook sword

44. 丁步崩剑 dīng bù bēng jiàn
flick sword up with T-step

45. 弓步点剑 gōng bù diǎn jiàn
bowstance and point sword

46. 翻腰抡劈剑 fān yāo lūn pī jiàn
rotate waist and chop sword

47. 扣腿刺剑 kòu tuǐ cì jiàn
pin back leg and thrust sword

48. 仆步摆剑 pū bù bǎi jiàn
crouch stance with sword above head

49. 插步劈剑 chā bù pī jiàn
cross legs and chop sword backward

50. 转身云接剑 zhuǎn shēn yún jiē jiàn
turn around and circle sword above head

51. 虚步持剑 xū bù chí jiàn
empty stance and hold sword

52. 前点步背剑上指 qián diǎn bù bèi jiàn shàng zhǐ
high empty stance with sword behind back and sword
fingers straight up

53. 收势 shōu shì
closing form

B Group Daoshu (Broad-Sword) Form
B 组刀术竞赛套路

Movements of B Group Daoshu (Broadsword)
B组刀术竞赛套路动作名称

第一段   **Part 1**

1.预备式 yù bèi shì
preparation form

2.抱刀右冲拳 bào dāo yòu chōng quán
hold broadsword and right hand punch

3.抱刀分手亮掌 bào dāo fēn shǒu liàng zhǎng
hold broadsword and palm upper block

4.单拍脚 dān pāi jiǎo
front slap kick

5.翻腰拍地 fān yāo pāi dì
rotate around waist and slap ground

6.剪腕花左右扎刀 jiǎn wàn huā zuǒ yòu zā dāo
circle broadsword around wrist and stab both sides

7.转身缠头刀 zhuǎn shēn chán tóu dāo
turn around and twine broadsword around
head from front

8.撩刀回身平扫 liāo dāo huí shēn píng sǎo
upward circle cut and turn back into horse stance
with horizontal slice

9.剪腕花分手点刀 jiǎn wàn huā fēn shǒu diǎn dāo
circle broadsword around wrist and open arms
pointing broadsword

10.缠头旋风腿 chán tóu xuán fēng tuǐ
twine broadsword around head from front into
tornado jump kick

11.马步藏刀 mǎ bù cáng dāo
horse stance and hide broadsword

12.并步斩刀 bìng bù zhǎn dāo
stand straight and cut broadsword shoulder level

13.缠头刀 chán tóu dāo
twine broadsword around head from front

14.剪腕花上扎刀 jiǎn wàn huā shàng zā dāo
circle broadsword arond wrist and thrust upward

15.弓步崩刀 gōng bù bēng dāo
bowstance and flick broadsword

第二段   **Part 2**

16.左挂刀 zuǒ guà dāo
hook broadsword on left side

17.上步撩刀 shàng bù liāo dāo
step forward and upper circle cut

18.剪腕花分手扎刀 jiǎn wàn huā fēn shǒu zā dāo
circle broadsword around wrist and thrust
broadsword with arms apart

19.回身上撩刀 huí shēn shàng liāo dāo
turn back and upper circle cut

20.抽身带刀 chōu shēn dài dāo
retract body and hold broadsword

21.错步扎刀 cuò bù zā dāo
bend with feet together and thrust broadsword

22.后推刀 hòu tuī dāo
push broadsword back with both hands

23.纵步下截刀 zòng bù xià jié dāo
hop and raise knee with diagonally downward chop

24.腾空左右扎刀 téng kōng zuǒ yòu zā dāo
jump and thrust broadsword on both sides

25.插步下截刀 chā bù xià jié dāo
cross legs and chop diagonally downward

26.转身云刀 zhuǎn shēn yún dāo
turn around and circle block above head
with broadsword

27.弓步分手扎刀 gōng bù fēn shǒu zā dāo
bowstance thrust with arms apart

第三段   Part 3
28.缠头刀 chán tóu dāo
twine broadsword around head from front

29.前点步错刀 qián diǎn bù cuò dāo
high empty stance and chop broadsword
horizontally at shoulder height

30.左右抡劈刀 zuǒ yòu lūn pī dāo
swinging chop broadsword on both sides

31.翻身抡劈刀 fān shēn lūn pī dāo
rotate body and swinging chop broadsword

33.旋转格刀 xuán zhuǎn gé dāo
spin body with broadsword blocking

34.弓步藏刀推掌 gōng bù cáng dāo tuī zhǎng
bowstance and hide staff with pushing palm

35.插步分手扎刀 chā bù fēn shǒu zā dāo
cross legs and thrust broadsword with arms apart

36.回身点刀 huí shēn diǎn dāo
turn back and point broadsword

37.扫刀旋子 sǎo dāo xuán zǐ
sweep broadsword and butterfly jump

38.云刀仰身推刀 yún dāo yǎng shēn tuī dāo
circle block with broadsword above head
and push broadsword

39.转身缠头刀 zhuǎn shēn chán tóu dāo
turn around and twine broadsword
around head from front

40.裹脑平抹刀 guǒ nǎo píng mǒ dāo
wrap broadsword around head from back
and horizontally slice

41.换跳步扎刀 huàn tiào bù zā dāo
jump and switch legs into bowstance thrust

第四段   **Part 4**
42.平分刀 píng fēn dāo
seperate arms and broadsword slice

43.云托按刀 yún tuō àn dāo
circle block broad sword above head and press

44.插步绞刀 chā bù jiǎo dāo
cross legs and circle broadsword

45.跪步推刀 guì bù tuī dāo
kneeling stance and push broadsword

46.纵步下截刀 zòng bù xià jié dāo
hop and raise knee with diagonally downward chop

47.上步扎刀 shàng bù zā dāo
step forward and thrust

48.撩腕花跳崩刀 liāo wàn huā tiào bēng dāo
upward circle broadsword around wrist
into broadsword flick and hop

49.分手点刀 fēn shǒu diǎn dāo
point broadsword with arms open

50.剪腕花并步扎刀 jiǎn wàn huā bìng bù zā dāo
circle broadsword around wrist into thrust
with feet together

51.崩刀前点 bēng dāo qián diǎn
flick broadsword and point forward

52.转身缠头刀 zhuǎn shēn chán tóu dāo
turn around twine broadsword around head

53.仆步下截刀 pū bù xià jié dāo
crouch stance and diagonally downward
chop broadsword

54.旋转缠脖刀 xuán zhuǎn chán bó dāo
turn body and twine broadsword around
neck from front

55.接刀弓步推掌 jiē dāo gōng bù tuī zhǎng
bowstance and grab broadsword
with pushing palm

56.左虚步切掌 zuǒ xū bù qiē zhǎng
left empty and chop with palm

57.并步按掌 bìng bù àn zhǎng
close feet and press hand down

58.并步收势 bìng bù shōu shì
closing form

B Group Gunshu (Staff) Form
B组棍术竞赛套路

Movements of B Group Gunshu(Staff)
B组棍术竞赛套路动作名称

第一段   **Part 1**

1.预备式 yù bèi shì
Preparation stance

2.撩掌推棍 liāo zhǎng tuī gùn
raise palm and push out staff

3.丁字步抱棍 dīng zì bù bào gùn
T-step and hold staff

4.平抡棍仆步抱棍 píng lūn gùn pū bù bào gùn
horizontally swing staff into crouch stance
and hold staff

5.歇步绞棍 xiē bù jiǎo gùn
cross leg stance and circle staff base

6.抢扫腾空举棍 lūn sǎo téng kōng jǔ gùn
sweep staff into jump with staff above head

7.仆步摔棍 pū bù shuāi gùn
crouch staff slam staff

8.抢棍弓步背棍 lūn gùn gōng bù bèi gùn
swing staff into bowstance with staff against back

9.转身云拨棍 zhuǎn shēn yún bō gùn
turn around and circle staff above head

10.转身抢棍 zhuǎn shēn lūn gùn
turn and swing staff

11.抢棍旋子 lūn gùn xuán zǐ
swing staff and butterfly jump

12.插步绞把 chā bù jiǎo bǎ
cross leg steps and rotate staff base

13.弓步戳把 gōng bù chuō bǎ
bowstance and hit with staff base

14.插步绞戳棍 chā bù jiǎo chuō gùn
cross leg steps and rotate staff into thrust

15.跳点棍仆步摔棍 tiào diǎn gùn pū bù shuāi gùn
hop while point staff to the left and right
into crouch stance slam

16.横裆步崩棍 héng dāng bù bēng gùn
sideways bowstance and flick staff upward

17.撩棍蹬腿 liāo gùn dēng tuǐ
circle staff diagonally upward and bend kick with heel

101

18.弓步戳把 gōng bù chuō bǎ
bowstance and hot with staff base

19.涮腰扫棍 shuàn yāo sǎo gùn
sweep staff above head and pivot body around waist

20.提膝背棍 tí xī bèi gùn
raise knee and hold staff on back

第二段　　　　　　　　**Part 2**

21.原地舞花 yuán dì wǔ huā
figure-eight spin staff in place

22.击步旋风脚 jī bù xuán fēng jiǎo
gallop into tornado jump kick

23.转身扫棍 zhuǎn shēn sǎo gùn
turn around and sweep staff

24.坐盘抱棍 zuò pán bào gùn
cross leg sit and hold staff

25.转身扫棍 zhuǎn shēn sǎo gùn
turn around and sweep staff

26.上步撩棍 shàng bù liāo gùn
step forward and swing staff diagonally upward

27.半马步劈棍 bàn mǎ bù pī gùn
chop downward on staff into half bowstance

28.弓步云拨棍 gōng bù yún bō gùn
circle block with staff above head into bowstance

29.扣腿戳把 kòu tuǐ chuō bǎ
pin back leg and hit with staff base

第三段　　　　　　　　　　Part 3

30.插步绞棍 chā bù jiǎo gùn
cross leg step and rotate staff base

31.插步戳棍 chā bù chuō gùn
cross legs and thrust staff head

32.舞花跳仆步摔棍 wǔ huā tiào pū bù shuāi gùn
swing staff and jump into crouch staff slam

33.弓步扫棍 gōng bù sǎo gùn
bowstance and sweep staff

34.转身跳点棍 zhuǎn shēn tiào diǎn gùn
turn around into hop and point staff

35.仆步摔棍 pū bù shuāi gùn
crouch stance and slam staff

36.转身盖把 zhuǎn shēn gài bǎ
turn around into a downward hit

37.抡棍弓步背棍 lūn gùn gōng bù bèi gùn
swing staff into bow stance with staff on back

第四段　　　　　　　　　　Part 4

38.转身点棍 zhuǎn shēn diǎn gùn
turn around and point staff on left and right sides

39.插步背棍 chā bù bèi gùn
cross legs with staff on back

40.插步云拨棍 chā bù yún bō gùn
cross legs and circle block with staff above head

41.转身抡扫棍 zhuǎn shēn lūn sǎo gùn
turn around and sweep with staff

42.跳仆步摔棍 tiào pū bù shuāi gùn
jump into crouch stance and slam staff

43.弓步崩棍 gōng bù bēng gùn
bow stance and flick staff head upward

44.插步绞棍 chā bù jiǎo gùn
cross legs and circle staff base

45.转身抡棍 zhuǎn shēn lūn gùn
turn around and swing staff

46.虚步背棍 xū bù bèi gùn
empty stance with staff on back

47.转身云棍 zhuǎn shēn yún gùn
turn around and circle block with staff above head

48.弓步推掌 gōng bù tuī zhǎng
bowstance and push palm

49.并步抱棍 bìng bù bào gùn
close feet and hold staff

50.收势 shōu shì
closing form

B Group Qiangshu (Spear) Form
B组枪术竞赛套路

Movements of B Group Qiangshu(Spear)
B组枪术竞赛套路动作名称

第一段   Part 1
1.预备式 yù bèi shì
preparation form

2.并步下扎枪 bìng bù xià zā qiāng
feet together and thrust downward with spear

3.插步亮掌 chā bù liàng zhǎng
cross legs and flip palm upward

4.转身弓步扎枪 zhuǎn shēn gōng bù zā qiāng
turn around into bow stance thrust spear

5.弓步拦拿扎枪 gōng bù lán ná zā qiāng
bow stance with outer and inner blocks
into spear thrust

6.后点步扎枪 hòu diǎn bù zā qiāng
back leg toe point on floor and spear thrust

7.跨步劈枪 kuà bù pī qiāng
large step forward and chop with spear

8.转身跃起劈枪 zhuǎn shēn yuè qǐ pī qiāng
turn and jump with spear chop

9.跨步托枪 kuà bù tuō qiāng
large step and block upward with spear above head

10.上步斜劈枪 shàng bù xié pī qiāng
step forward and chop diagonally with spear

11.插步下拨枪 chā bù xià bō qiāng
cross legs step and lower spear block

12.并步半蹲下扎枪 bìng bù bàn dūn xià zā qiāng
feet together with slight bend and thrust

13.转身劈枪 zhuǎn shēn pī qiāng
turn around and spear chop

14.转身拦拿扎枪 zhuǎn shēn lán ná zā qiāng
turn around with outer and inner blocks
into spear thrust

15.弓步拦拿扎枪 gōng bù lán ná zā qiāng
bow stance with outer and inner blocks
into spear thrust

16.横裆步托枪 héng dāng bù tuō qiāng
sideways bow stance and upper block with spear

17.转身劈枪 zhuǎn shēn pī qiāng
turn around and chop with spear

18.高虚步抱枪 gāo xū bù bào qiāng
high empty stance and hold spear

第二段   **Part 2**
19.后点步扎枪 hòu diǎn bù zā qiāng
back leg toe point on floor and spear thrust

20.上步劈枪 shàng bù pī qiāng
step forward and spear chop

21.横裆步上托枪 héng dāng bù shàng tuō qiāng
sideways bowstance and upper block with spear

22.转身扣腿点枪 zhuǎn shēn kòu tuǐ diǎn qiāng
turn around into spear point with pinned leg

23.并步崩枪 bìng bù bēng qiāng
feet together and flip staff point upward

24.弧形步绞枪 hú xíng bù jiǎo qiāng
crescent steps and rotate spear base

25.插步拦拿扎枪 chā bù lán ná zā qiāng
cross steps with outer and inner spear blocks

26.盖步拦拿扎枪 gài bù lán ná zā qiāng
cover step with outer and inner spear blocks

27.弓步拦拿扎枪 gōng bù lán ná zā qiāng
bow stance with outer and inner spear blocks

28.反身下扎枪 fǎn shēn xià zā qiāng
turn around and thrust spear downward

29.弓步侧推掌 gōng bù cè tuī zhǎng
bowstance and push palm diagonally

30.虚步崩枪 xū bù bēng qiāng
empty stance and flip spear head upward

31.左右舞花枪 zuǒ yòu wǔ huā qiāng
circle block with spear on left and right sides

32.舞花过背枪 wǔ huā guò bèi qiāng
circle spear around back

33.云枪拿扎枪 yún qiāng ná zā qiāng
circle block with spear above head into inner block and
spear thrust

34.反手穿梭枪 fǎn shǒu chuān suō qiāng
twist hand and shoot spear base through hand

35.回身绕喉穿枪 huí shēn rào hóu chuān qiāng
turn around and shoot spear head in front of neck

36.跟步劈枪 gēn bù pī qiāng
spear chop with feet together and slight bend

37.回身劈枪 huí shēn pī qiāng
turn around and spear chop

38.单手抛枪 dān shǒu pāo qiāng
throw and catch spear with one hand

39.仆步摔把 pū bù shuāi bǎ
crouch stance and slam spear base

40.抛枪 pāo qiāng
throw spear

41.转身坐盘抱枪 zhuǎn shēn zuò pán bào qiāng
turn around into cross leg sit and hold spear

42.转身拦拿扎枪 zhuǎn shēn lán ná zā qiāng
turn around into outer and inner spear block

43.弓步拦拿扎枪 gōng bù lán ná zā qiāng
bow stance with outer and inner block into spear thrust

44.丁步崩枪 dīng bù bēng qiāng
t-step and flip spear head upward

45.挑枪戳把 tiāo qiāng chuō bǎ
flip spear base upward and hit with spear base

46.翻身过背舞花枪 fān shēn guò bèi wǔ huā qiāng
turn around and circle spear around body

47.转身提膝下扎枪 zhuǎn shēn tí xī xià zā qiāng
turn around and jump with raised knee and spear thrust downward

48.云枪拿扎枪 yún qiāng ná zā qiāng
circle block with spear above head into inner block and spear thrust

49.弓步拦拿扎枪 gōng bù lán ná zā qiāng
bow stance with outer and inner block into spear thrust

50.横裆步托枪 héng dāng bù tuō qiāng
sideways bow stance and upper block with spear

51.横裆步斜举枪 héng dāng bù xié jǔ qiāng
sideways bow stance and raise spear diagonally

52.并步立枪推掌 bìng bù lì qiāng tuī zhǎng
hold spear vertically with feet together and push palm
diagonally

53.收势 shōu shì
closing form

B Group Nanquan (Southern Style Barehand) Form
B组南拳竞赛套路

Movements of B Group Nanquan
B组南拳竞赛套路动作名称

第一段　　　　　　　　　**Part 1**

1.预备势 yù bèi shì
preparation stance

2.并步抱拳 bìng bù bào quán
hold fists with feet together

3.抱拳震脚 bào quán zhèn jiǎo
hold fists and stomp

4.左弓步冲拳 zuǒ gōng bù chōng quán
left bow stance punch

5.左弓步冲拳 zuǒ gōng bù chōng quán
left bow stance punch

6.高虚步鞭拳 gāo xū bù biān quán
high empty stance and whip fist

7.骑龙步冲拳 qí lóng bù chōng quán
dragon-riding stance and punch

8.左弓步冲拳 zuǒ gōng bù chōng quán
left bow stance punch

9.左弓步截桥 zuǒ gōng bù jié qiáo
left bow stance and block with forearm

10.左弓步圈桥标掌 zuǒ gōng bù quān qiáo biāo zhǎng
left bow stance and circle forearm into
thrust with flat palm

11.马步双切掌 mǎ bù shuāng qiē zhǎng
horse stance with double palm chop

12.马步左右挑掌 mǎ bù zuǒ yòu tiāo zhǎng
horse stance with left and right palm flip

13.马步双推单指 mǎ bù shuāng tuī dān zhǐ
horse stance and push both pointer palms

14.马步双推单指 mǎ bù shuāng tuī dān zhǐ
horse stance and push both pointer palms

15.马步双标掌沉桥
mǎ bù shuāng biāo zhǎng chén qiáo
horse stance and thrust both palms vertically with
fingers forward and sink forearms

16.左弓步架桥 zuǒ gōng bù jià qiáo
left bow stance and block upward with forearms

17.骑龙步压肘 qí lóng bù yā zhǒu
dragon-riding stance and press with elbow

18.开步双虎爪 kāi bù shuāng hǔ zhǎo
stand with feet apart and both hands tiger claws

19.骑龙步推掌 qí lóng bù tuī zhǎng
dragon-riding stance and push palm

20.腾空转体里合腿 téng kōng zhuǎn tǐ lǐ hé tuǐ
inside turning jump kick

21.跌扑剪扫侧踹腿 diē pū jiǎn sǎo cè chuài tuǐ
lay on side and both legs scissor kick into upward kick

22.鲤鱼打挺 lǐ yú dǎ tǐng
kick up

23.虚步鹤嘴手 xū bù hè zuǐ shǒu
empty stance with crane beak hands

24.独立步双虎爪 dú lì bù shuāng hǔ zhǎo
stand on one leg with both hands tiger claw

25.左弓步双虎爪 zuǒ gōng bù shuāng hǔ zhǎo
left bow stance with both hands tiger claw

26.转身鞭拳插掌 zhuǎn shēn biān quán chā zhǎng
turn around into whip fist and thrust palm vertically
with fingers forward

27.前蹬腿冲拳 qián dēng tuǐ chōng quán
forward bend kick with heel and punch

28.跪步盖拳 guì bù gài quán
kneeling stance and fist doward swing

29.骑龙步撞拳 qí lóng bù zhuàng quán
dragon-riding stance and fist uppercut

30.马步劈桥 mǎ bù pī qiáo
horse stance and horizontal forearm chop

第二段   **Part 2**
31.转身挂盖拳 zhuǎn shēn guà gài quán
turn around and downward swing block hit with fists

32.横钉腿右弓步冲拳
héng dīng tuǐ yòu gōng bù chōng quán
diagonal nail kick into right bow stance and punch

33.勒手横踩腿双推掌
lè shǒu héng cǎi tuǐ shuāng tuī zhǎng
grab and low kick into horizontal chop with palms

34.单蝶步拍地 dān dié bù pāi dì
single butterfly stance and slam ground

35.右弓步叠掌 yòu gōng bù dié zhǎng
right bow stance with butterfly palms

36.麒麟步左弓步叠掌 qí lín bù zuǒ gōng bù dié zhǎng
Qilin steps into left bow stance with butterfly palms

37.右弓步架冲拳 yòu gōng bù jià chōng quán
right bowstance with upper block and punch

38.左横档步右抛拳 zuǒ héng dàng bù yòu pāo quán
right fist swing upward into left sideways bow stance

39.右横档步左抛拳 yòu héng dàng bù zuǒ pāo quán
left fist swing upward into right sideways bow stance

40.上步挂盖拳 shàng bù guà gài quán
step forward and downward swinging block
hit with fists

41.插步鞭拳 chā bù biān quán
cross leg steps and whip fist

42.转身挂盖拳 zhuǎn shēn guà gài quán
turn around and downward swinging block
hit with fists

43.拖步抛撞拳 tuō bù pāo zhuàng quán
step and drag back leg forward with uppercut fist

44.马步撑掌 mǎ bù chēng zhǎng
horse stance and chop with palms

45.挂盖扫右弓步撞拳
guà gài sǎo yòu gōng bù zhuàng quán
downward swing block hit and horizoontally fist and
open hit with both fists

46.歇步下冲拳 xiē bù xià chōng quán
cross leg stance and punch downward

47.马步双挂拳 mǎ bù shuāng guà quán
horse stance and split both fists outward

48.跪步双虎爪 guì bù shuāng hǔ zhǎo
kneeling stance with both hands tiger claws

第三段   Part 3
49.单拍脚半马步冲拳
dān pāi jiǎo bàn mǎ bù chōng quán
single front slap kick into shifted horse stance
with punch

50.单蝶步压肘 dān dié bù yā zhǒu
single butterfly stance and press elbow

51.插步冲拳 chā bù chōng quán
cross step and punch

52.上步冲拳转身挂盖拳
shàng bù chōng quán zhuǎn shēn guà gài quán
step forward punch and turn around into downward
swinging block hit with fists

53.马步侧冲拳 mǎ bù cè chōng quán
horse stance and sideways punch

第四段   Part 4
54.转身挂盖右弓步滚桥
zhuǎn shēn guà gài yòu gōng bù gǔn qiáo
turn around into downward swinging block hit and
right bowstance with twisted forearm

55.右弓步双推单指 yòu gōng bù shuāng tuī dān zhǐ
right bow stance and push both pointer palms

56.上步挂盖拳 shàng bù guà gài quán
step forward with downward swinging block hit

57.拖步抛撞拳 tuō bù pāo zhuàng quán
step and drag back foot forward with uppercut

58.拖步冲拳 tuō bù chōng quán
step and drag back foot forward with punch

59.插步鞭拳转身挂盖拳
chā bù biān quán zhuǎn shēn guà gài quán
cross step whip fist and turn around into
downward swinging block hit with fists

60.弓步架掌 gōng bù jià zhǎng
bow stance and upper block with palms

61.转身挂盖退步冲拳
zhuǎn shēn guà gài tuì bù chōng quán
turn around into downward swinging block hit
and step back punch

62.左弓步双推掌 zuǒ gōng bù shuāng tuī zhǎng
left bow stance and push both palms

63.虚步推掌冲拳 xū bù tuī zhǎng chōng quán
empty stance with pushing palm and punch

64.并步抱拳 bìng bù bào quán
feet together and hold fists

65.收势 shōu shì
closing form

B Group Nandao (Southern Style Broadsword) Form
B组南刀竞赛套路

Movements of B Group Nandao
B组南刀竞赛套路动作名称

第一段   **Part 1**
预备式 yù bèi shì
preparation form

1.虚步抱刀 xū bù bào dāo
empty stance and hold Nandao

2.骑龙步带刀 qí lóng bù dài dāo
dragon-riding stance and retract Nandao

3.上步左右砍刀 shàng bù zuǒ yòu kǎn dāo
step forward with Nandao chops on left and right sides

4.弓步推刀 gōng bù tuī dāo
bow stance and push Nandao

5.横档步立捧刀 héng dàng bù lì pěng dāo
sideways bow stance and hold Nandao vertically

6.上步左右横砍 shàng bù zuǒ yòu héng kǎn
step forward and horizontally on left and right sides

7.单蝶步挫刀 dān dié bù cuò dāo
single butterfly stance and horizontally
chop with Nandao

8.马步撩架 mǎ bù liāo jià
horse stance with upper circle bock

9.丁步按刀 dīng bù àn dāo
t-step and press Nandao downward

10.旋风脚 xuán fēng jiǎo
buttery jump

11.单蝶步扎刀 dān dié bù zā dāo
single butterfly stance and thrust Nandao

12.左扫右抹刀 zuǒ sǎo yòu mǒ dāo
sweep Nandao left and slide Nandao right

13.提膝挂刀 tí xī guà dāo
raise knee and circle hook Nandao on both sides

14.骑龙步格刀 qí lóng bù gé dāo
dragon-riding stance and downward block
with Nandao

15.骑龙步架刀 qí lóng bù jià dāo
dragon-riding stance and upper block with Nandao

16.上步劈刀 shàng bù pī dāo
step forward and chop with Nandaao

17.骑龙步下截刀 qí lóng bù xià jié dāo
dragon-riding stance and lower block with Nandao

18.麒麟步剪腕花 qí lín bù jiǎn wàn huā
Qilin steps and rotate Nandao with wrist

19.横档步立推刀 héng dàng bù lì tuī dāo
sideways bow stance and push vertical Nandao

第二段　　　　　　　　　　　Part 2

20.马步撩刀 mǎ bù liāo dāo
horse stance and upper circle block with Nandao

21.弓步撩刀 gōng bù liāo dāo
bowstance and circle block with Nandao

22.回身提膝挫刀 huí shēn tí xī cuò dāo
turn around and raise knee with forward block

23.跳转身单蝶步砍刀
tiào zhuǎn shēn dān dié bù kǎn dāo
turn and jump into single butterfly stance
with Nandao chop

24.马步撩刀 mǎ bù liāo dāo
horse stance and upper circle block with Nandao

25.弓步格刀 gōng bù gé dāo
bow stance and block with Nandao

26.插步反把扎刀 chā bù fǎn bǎ zā dāo
cross leg step and thrust Nandao backward

27.退步抹刀 tuì bù mǒ dāo
step back and slide Nandao blade on both sides

28.回身上步左右劈刀
huí shēn shàng bù zuǒ yòu pī dāo
turn around and chop Nanda on left and right sides

29.马步劈刀 mǎ bù pī dāo
horse stance Nandao chop

30.跳转身马步砍刀 tiào zhuǎn shēn mǎ bù kǎn dāo
turn and jump into horse stance with downward
Nandao chop

31.提膝扎刀 tí xī zā dāo
raise knee and thrust Nandao

第三段   Part 3
32.马步崩刀 mǎ bù bēng dāo
horse stance and flick Nandao point upward

33.弓步挫刀 gōng bù cuò dāo
bow stance and forward block with Nandao

34.马步截刀 mǎ bù jié dāo
horse stance with Nandao block

35.转身弓步云抹刀 zhuǎn shēn gōng bù yún mǒ dāo
turn around with circle block and Nandao slide
into bow stance

36.转身骑龙步云抹刀
zhuǎn shēn qí lóng bù yún mǒ dāo
turn around with circle block and Nandao slide
into dragon-riding stance

37.弓步扎刀 gōng bù zā dāo
bow stance Nandao thrust

38.上步穿刀 shàng bù chuān dāo
step forward and pierce Nandao

39.半马步截刀 bàn mǎ bù jié dāo
shifted horse stance with lower Nandao block

40.撩腕花 liāo wàn huā
Nandao upward circle block with wrist

41.翻身跳仆步劈刀 fān shēn tiào pū bù pī dāo
turn and jump into crouch stance chop

42.剪腕花 jiǎn wàn huā
Nandao downward circle with wrist

43.抹刀后摆腿 mǒ dāo hòu bǎi tuǐ
slide Nandao and swing leg backward

44.单蝶步反抹刀 dān dié bù fǎn mǒ dāo
single butterfly whip and slide Nandao

45.马步反手扎刀 mǎ bù fǎn shǒu zā dāo
horse stance and thrust Nandao with elbow forward

46.半马步立推刀 bàn mǎ bù lì tuī dāo
shifted horse stance and push vertical Nandao

47.提膝挂刀 tí xī guà dāo
raise knee and hook circle Nandao on both sides

48.跳转身背花 tiào zhuǎn shēn bèi huā
turn and jump into circle Nandao with wrist
behind back

49.弓步带刀 gōng bù dài dāo
bow stance and retract Nandao

第四段 Part 4

50.上步撩刀 shàng bù liāo dāo
step forward and upper circle block with Nandao

51.插步撩刀 chā bù liāo dāo
cross leg step and upper circle block with Nandao

52.弓步扎刀 gōng bù zā dāo
bow stance thrust with Nandao

53.马步截刀 mǎ bù jié dāo
horse stance with Nandao block

54.背刀 bèi dāo
swing Nandao upward behind back

55.左右扫刀 zuǒ yòu sǎo dāo
sweep Nandao left and right

56.回身撩刀 huí shēn liāo dāo
turn around and upper circle Nandao block

57.左右扫刀 zuǒ yòu sǎo dāo
sweep Nandao left and right

58.跳转身骑龙步砍刀
tiào zhuǎn shēn qí lóng bù kǎn dāo
turn and jump into dragon-riding stance
with Nandao chop

59.弓步带刀 gōng bù dài dāo
bow stance and retract Nandao

60.上步砍刀 shàng bù kǎn dāo
step forward and Nandao chop

61.马步砍刀 mǎ bù kǎn dāo
horse stance and Nandao chop

62.跳转身马步砍刀 tiào zhuǎn shēn mǎ bù kǎn dāo
turn and jump into horse stance with Nandao chop

63.弓步斩刀 gōng bù zhǎn dāo
bow stance and Nandao upper block

64.盖步截刀 gài bù jié dāo
cover step with Nandao block

65.跪步推刀 guì bù tuī dāo
kneeling stance and push Nandao

66.半马步抱刀 bàn mǎ bù bào dāo
shifted horsestance and hold Nandao

收势 shōu shì
closing form

B Group Nangun (Southern Style Staff) Form
B组南棍竞赛套路

Movements of B Group Nangun
B组南棍竞赛套路动作名称

第一段	Part 1

预备式 yù bèi shì
Preparation form

1.左虚步盖掌 zuǒ xū bù gài zhǎng
left empty stance and cover with palm

2.右弓步斜抱棍 yòu gōng bù xié bào gùn
right bow stance and hold Nangun diagonally

3.左弓步劈棍（发声: 嘿）
zuǒ gōng bù pī gùn （fā shēng: hēi)
left bow stance and Nangun chop (shout: hey)

4.马步戳棍 mǎ bù chuō gùn
horse stance and Nangun thrust

125

5.马步滚压棍 mǎ bù gǔn yā gùn
horse stance and rotate Nangun into downward press

6.拐步下拨棍 guǎi bù xià bō gùn
cross steps and block Nangun downward

7.马步戳棍 mǎ bù chuō gùn
horse stance and Nangun thrust

8.马步滚压棍 mǎ bù gǔn yā gùn
horse stance and rotate Nangun into downward press

9.转身左弓步下拨棍
zhuǎn shēn zuǒ gōng bù xià bō gùn
turn around into left bow stance and block
Nangun downward

10.左弓步盖棍 zuǒ gōng bù gài gùn
left bow stance and hit Nangun top dowm

11.左弓步斜击棍 zuǒ gōng bù xié jī gùn
left bow stance and hit Nangun diagonally upward

12.马步挑把 mǎ bù tiāo bǎ
horse stance and flip Nangun base upward

13.左骑龙步斜击棍 zuǒ qí lóng bù xié jī gùn
left dragon-riding stance and hit Nangun diagonally to
the side

14.右骑龙步斜把 yòu qí lóng bù xié jī bǎ
right dragon-riding stance and hit Nangun base diagonally to the side

15.上步左格棍 shàng bù zuǒ gé gùn
step forward and block with Nangun vertically
to the left

16.上步右格棍 shàng bù yòu gé gùn
step forward and block with Nangun vertically
to the right

17.跳步左弓步斜击棍 tiào bù zuǒ gōng bù xié jī gùn
hop into left bow stance and hit Nangun diagonally

18.半马步挂劈棍 bàn mǎ bù guà pī gùn
hook Nangun downward into chop with
shifted horse stance

19.半马步戳棍 bàn mǎ bù chuō gùn
shifted horse stance and thrust Nangun

20.前跃半马步戳棍 qián yuè bàn mǎ bù chuō gùn
jump forward into shifted horse stance and
thrust Nangun

第二段   **Part 2**
21.盖步左弓步绞压棍 gài bù zuǒ gōng bù jiǎo yā gùn
forward step into left bow stance and rotate Nangun
into downward press

22.半马步挑劈棍（发声：嗨）
bàn mǎ bù tiāo pī gùn (fā shēng: hāi)
shifted horse stance and flip Nangun upward into
downward chop (shout: hai)

23.回身左弓步戳把 huí shēn zuǒ gōng bù chuō bǎ
turn around into left bow stance and thrust Nangun

24.左弓步挂劈棍 zuǒ gōng bù guà pī gùn
hook Nangun downward into chop with left bowstance

25.跳步跪步右云拨棍 tiào bù guì bù yòu yún bō gùn
hop and circle block Nangun above head into right
kneeling stance with Nangun block

26.跳步跪步左云拨棍 tiào bù guì bù zuǒ yún bō gùn
hop and circle block Nangun above head into left
kneeling stance with Nangun block

27.上步撩把 shàng bù liāo bǎ
forward steps and circle block the sides with
Nangun base

28.上步撩棍 shàng bù liāo gùn
forward steps and circle block the sides with
Nangun head

29.上步撩把 shàng bù liāo bǎ
forward steps and circle block the sides with
Nangun base

30.左弓步斜击棍 zuǒ gōng bù xié jī gùn
left bow stance and hit Nangun diagonally upward

31.丁腿斜击把 dīng tuǐ xié jī bǎ
diagonal nail kick and hit Nangun diagonally upward

32.左弓步斜击棍 zuǒ gōng bù xié jī gùn
left bow stance and hit Nangun diagonally upward

33.马步挂劈棍 mǎ bù guà pī gùn
hook Nangun downward into chop with horse stance

34.上步马步挑棍 shàng bù mǎ bù tiāo gùn
step forward into horse stance and flip
Nangun upward

35.马步挂劈棍 mǎ bù guà pī gùn
hook Nangun downward into chop with horse stance

36.回身左弓步斜击棍 huí shēn zuǒ gōng bù xié jī gùn
turn around into left bow stance and hit
Nangun diagonally upward

第三段　　　　　　　　Part 3
37.右弓步戳把 yòu gōng bù chuō bǎ
right bow stance and thrust Nangun base

38.左弓步下弹棍 zuǒ gōng bù xià dàn gùn
left bow stance and block Nangun downward

39.右弓步格把 yòu gōng bù gé bǎ
right bow stance and block with Nangun base

40.左弓步斜击棍 zuǒ gōng bù xié jī gùn
left bow stance and hit Nangun diagonally upward

41.转身马步云拨棍 zhuǎn shēn mǎ bù yún bō gùn
turn around and circle block Nangun above head into
horse stance with Nangun block

42.跳转身左弓步推棍（发声：嗳）
tiào zhuǎn shēn zuǒ gōng bù tuī gùn (fā shēng: ǎi)
turn and jump into left bow stance with Nangun push
(shout: ai)

43.转身左弓步劈棍 zhuǎn shēn zuǒ gōng bù pī gùn
turn around into left bow stance and Nangun chop

44.麒麟步马步云拨棍 qí lín bù mǎ bù yún bō gùn
Qilin steps and circle block Nangun above head into
horse stance with Nangun block

45.半马步绞崩棍 bàn mǎ bù jiǎo bēng gùn
shifted horse stance and rotate head into upward flick

46.右弓步下拨棍 yòu gōng bù xià bō gùn
right bow stance and downward Nangun block

47.上步右虚步崩棍 shàng bù yòu xū bù bēng gùn
forward steps into right empty stance and
upward Nangun flick

第四段　　　　　　　　　**Part 4**
48.回身提膝上挑棍 huí shēn tí xī shàng tiāo gùn
turn around into upward Nangun hit with raised knee

49.右虚步下拨棍 yòu xū bù xià bō gùn
right empty stance and downward Nangun block

50.左弓步抱棍 zuǒ gōng bù bào gùn
left bow stance and hit Nangun upward

51.提膝柱棍 tí xī zhù gùn
raise knee and plant staff vertically on ground

52.左右舞花棍 zuǒ yòu wǔ huā gùn
circle block staff on the left and right sides

53.跳翻身仆步摔棍 tiào fān shēn pū bù shuāi gùn
turn and jump into crouch stance with Nangun slam

54.骑龙步顶棍 qí lóng bù dǐng gùn
dragon-riding stance and hold Nangun head up
with base on ground

55.盖步绞棍 gài bù jiǎo gùn
front cross step and rotate Nangun head

56.右弓步戳棍 yòu gōng bù chuō gùn
right bow stance and Nangun thrust

57.拖步斜击把 tuō bù xié jī bǎ
step and drag back leg forward with diagonal Nangun base hit upward

58.拖步斜击棍 tuō bù xié jī gùn
step and drag back leg forward with diagonal Nangun head hit upward

59.拖步下击把 tuō bù xià jī bǎ
step and drag back leg forward with diagonal Nangun base hit upward

60.左弓步劈棍 zuǒ gōng bù pī gùn
left bowstance and Nangun chop

61.跳转身单蝶步摔棍
tiào zhuǎn shēn dān dié bù shuāi gùn
turn and jump into single butterfly stance with Nangun slam

62.右弓步斜后挂棍 yòu gōng bù xié hòu guà gùn
right bow stance and hook Nangun diagonally backward

63.右弓步劈棍 yòu gōng bù pī gùn
right bow stance and Nangun chop

64.转身左弓步斜击棍
zhuǎn shēn zuǒ gōng bù xié jī gùn
turn around into left bow stance and diagonally hit Nangun upward

65.左弓步平推棍（发声：嗳）
zuǒ gōng bù píng tuī gùn (fā shēng: ǎi)
left bow stance and push horizontal Nangun forward (shout: ai)

66.左虚步抽棍 zuǒ xū bù chōu gùn
left empty stance and retract Nangun

收势 shōu shì
closing form

B Group TaijiQuan (42 form Tai Chi) Form
B 组太极拳竞赛套路 (42式太极拳)

Movements of B Group TaijiQuan42 Form Tai Chi
B组太极拳竞赛套路动作名称

第一段   **Part 1**

1.起势qǐ shì
Commencing form

2.右揽雀尾 yòu lǎn què wěi
Right grasp the peacock's tail

3.左单鞭 zuǒ dān biān
Left single whip

4.提手tí shǒu
Lift hands

5.白鹤亮翅 bái hè liàng chì
White crane spreads wings

6.搂膝拗步 lǒu xī ǎo bù
Brush knee and twist steps on both sides

7.撇身捶 piē shēn chuí
Dodge body and throw fist

8.捋挤势 luō jǐ shì
Deflect and squeeze

9.进步搬拦捶 jìn bù bān lán chuí
 Step forward, parry and punch

10.如封似闭 rú fēng sì bì
Apparent close up

第二段   Part 2

11.开合手 kāi hé shǒu
Open and close hands

12.右单鞭 yòu dān biān
Right single whip

13.肘底捶 zhǒu dǐ chuí
Fist under elbow

14.转身推掌 zhuǎn shēn tuī zhǎng
Turn body and push palm

15.玉女穿梭 yù nǚ chuān suō
Fair lady working with shuttles on both sides

16.左右蹬脚 zuǒ yòu dēng jiǎo
Kick with heel on both sides

17.掩手肱捶 yǎn shǒu gōng chuí
Hide hands and strike fist

18.野马分鬃 yě mǎ fēn zōng
Parting the wild horse's mane on both sides

第三段   **Part 3**
19.云手 yún shǒu
Wave hands like clouds

20.独立打虎 dú lì dǎ hǔ
Beat tiger on single leg

21.右分脚 yòu fēn jiǎo
Right toes kick

22.双峰贯耳 shuāng fēng guàn ěr
Striking the opponent's ears with both fists

23.左分脚 zuǒ fēn jiǎo
Left toes kick

24.转身拍脚 zhuǎn shēn pāi jiǎo
Turn body and slap foot

25.进步栽捶 jìn bù zāi chuí
Step Forward and punch down

26.斜飞势 xié fēi shì
Flying obliquely

27.单鞭下势 dān biān xià shì
Single whip Lower Position

28.金鸡独立 jīn jī dú lì
Golden rooster stands on one leg

29.退步穿掌 tuì bù chuān zhǎng
Step back and pierce palm

30.虚步压掌 xū bù yā zhǎng
Press palm with empty stance

31.独立托掌 dú lì tuō zhǎng
Stand on one leg and raise palm

32.马步靠 mǎ bù kào
Lean and horse stance

33.转身大将 zhuǎn shēn dà luō
Turn body and deflect

34.歇步擒打 xiē bù qín dǎ
Cross legged sitting stance and lock strike

35.穿掌下势 chuān zhǎng xià shì
Pierce palm and push down

36.上步七星 shàng bù qī xīng
Step forward with seven stars

37.退步跨虎 tuì bù kuà hǔ
Back step and straddle the tiger

38.转身摆莲 zhuǎn shēn bǎi lián
Turn body and lotus kick

39.弯弓射虎 wān gōng shè hǔ
Bend bow to shoot tiger

40.左揽雀尾 zuǒ lǎn què wěi
Left grasp the peacock's tail

41.十字手 shí zì shǒu
Cross hands

42.收势 shōu shì
Closing form

B Group TaijiJian (Tai Chi Sword) Form
B组太极剑竞赛套路

Movements of B Group TaijiJian(42 Form Tai Chi Sowrd) B组太极剑竞赛套路动作名称

第一段   **Part 1**

1.起势 qǐ shì
Commencing form

2.并步点剑 bìng bù diǎn jiàn
Stand with feet together and point sword

3.弓步削剑 gōng bù xiāo jiàn
Bow stance and cut obliquely

4.提膝劈剑 tí xī pī jiàn
Lift knee and chop sword

5.左弓步拦 zuǒ gōng bù lán
Left bow stance and parry sword

6.左虚步撩 zuǒ xū bù liāo
Left empty stance and cut upward sword

7.右弓步撩 yòu gōng bù liāo
Right bow stance and cut upward with sword

8.提膝捧剑 tí xī pěng jiàn
Lift knee and hold sword in both hands

9.蹬脚前刺 dēng jiǎo qián cì
Heel kick and thrust sword

10.跳步平刺 tiào bù píng cì
Jump step and thrust sword

11.转身下刺 zhuǎn shēn xià cì
Turn body and thrust downward

第二段   **Part 2**
12.弓步平斩 gōng bù píng zhǎn
Bow stance and cut horizontally

13.弓步崩剑 gōng bù bēng jiàn
Bow stance and tilt sword

14.歇步压剑 xiē bù yā jiàn
Rest stance and press sword

15.进步绞剑 jìn bù jiǎo jiàn
Advance and circle with sword

16.提膝上刺 tí xī shàng cì
Lift knee and thrust sword

17.虚步下截 xū bù xià jié
Empty stance to intercept with sword

18.右左平带　yòu zuǒ píng dài
Withdraw sword to both sides

19.弓步劈剑　gōng bù pī jiàn
Bow stance and chop sword

20.丁步托剑　dīng bù tuō jiàn
T-stance and hold sword upblock

21.分脚后点　fēn jiǎo hòu diǎn
Right Toes kick and point sword backward

第三段　　　　　　　　**Part 3**

22.右仆步穿剑　pú bù chuān jiàn
Crouch stance and thrust sword

23.左蹬脚架剑　dēng jiǎo jià jiàn
Left heel kick and sword upblock

24.左提膝点剑　zuǒ tí xī diǎn jiàn
Lift knee and sword point downward

25.仆步横扫　pú bù héng sǎo
Crouch stance and sweep sword

26.右 左弓步下截　gōng bù xià jié
Bow stance and intercept on both sides

27.弓步下刺　gōng bù xià cì
Bow stance and thrust sword

28.右左云抹　yòu zuǒ yún mǒ
Wave sword on both sides

29.右弓步劈　yòu gōng bù pī
Right bow stance and chop sword

30.后举腿架剑 hòu jǔ tuǐ jià jiàn
Raise leg backward and block

31.丁步点剑 dīng bù diǎn jiàn
T-stance and point sword

32.马步推剑 mǎ bù tuī jiàn
Horse stance and push sword

第四段   **Part 4**
33.独立上托 dú lì shàng tuō
Stand on one leg and hold up sword

34.进步挂剑 jìn bù guà jiàn
Advance to parry and point

35.歇步崩剑 xiē bù bēng jiàn
Cross stance and tilt sword

36.弓步反刺 gōng bù fǎn cì
Bow stance and back thrust sword

37.转身下刺 zhuǎn shēn xià cì
Turn body and thrust sword

38.提膝提剑 tí xī tí jiàn
Lift knee and sword

39.行步穿剑 xíng bù chuān jiàn
Walk and pierce sword

40.摆腿云剑 bǎi tuǐ yún jiàn
Outside kick with sword circle block

41.弓步架剑 gōng bù jià jiàn
Bow stance sword block

42.弓步直刺 gōng bù zhí cì
Bow stance and thrust sword

42.收势 shōu shì
Closing form

Optional Taijishan Routine (Without Degree of Difficulty Movements)
自选太极扇套路(无难度)

第一段   **Part 1**

1.起势 qǐ shì
opening form

2.金刚捣锥 jīn gāng dǎo zhuī
warrior attendant pounding mortar

3.懒扎衣 lǎn zhā yī
lazily tying the coat

4.六封四闭 liù fēng sì bì
six sealing and four closing

5.开扇抛接 kāi shàn pāo jiē
open fan front toss and catch

6.单鞭 dān biān
single whip

7.前招 qián zhāo
maneuver to the front

8.后招 hòu zhāo
maneuver to the rear

9.贴身靠 tiē shēn kào
leaning body on the diagonal

10.白鹤亮翅 bái hè liàng chì
white crane spreads its wings

11.斜行 xié xíng
flying diagonally

12.提收 tí shōu
defending from a kick

13.射雁式 shè yàn shì
shooting wild geese

14.海底捞月 hǎi dǐ lāo yuè
scooping up the moon from beneath the sea

15.掩手肱捶 lǎn shǒu gōng chuí
strike with concealed fist

16.穿心肘 chuān xīn zhǒu
piercing the heart elbow strike

17.青龙出水 qīng lóng chū shuǐ
black dragon comes out of the water

18.怪蟒翻身 guài mǎng fān shēn
monstrous serpent flips over

19.燕子啄泥 yàn zi zhuó ní
sparrow pecks the mud)

第二段   **Part 2**
20.大鹏展翅 dà péng zhǎnchì
great bird spreads its wings

21.海底翻花 hǎi dǐ fān huā
turning over flowers from the bottom of the sea

22.二起脚 èr qǐ jiǎo
jumping front slap kick

23.双震脚 shuāng zhèn jiǎo
stamping with both feet

24.蹬一根 dēng yī gēn
kicking root

25.玉女穿梭 yù nǚ chuān suō
fair lady works the shuttle

26.摘星换斗 zhāi xīng huàn dòu
plucking the stars to change the constellations

27.乌龙翻身 wū lóng fān shēn
black dragon flips over

28.罗汉降龙 luó hàn xiáng lóng
Arhat subdues the dragon

29.饿虎扑食 è hǔ pū shí
hungry tiger pounces on its prey

30.抱虎推山 bào hǔ tuī shān
embrace the tiger and push the mountain

31.云手 yún shǒu
cloud hands

32.伏虎式 fú hǔ shì
taming the tiger movement

33.金刚捣锥 jīn gāng dǎo zhuī
warrior attendant pounding mortar

34.收势 shōu shì
closing form

A Group Changquan (Barehand) Form
A组长拳竞赛套路

预备势 yù bèi shì
preparation stance

第一段   **Part 1**
1.虚步亮掌 xū bù liàng zhǎng
empty stance with palm and hook

2.上步对拳 shàng bù duì quán
step forward and drag fists downward

3.弓步撩推掌 gōng bù liāo tuī zhǎng
bow stance and circle palm toward body into push

4.弹腿击掌 dàn tuǐ jī zhǎng
push palm and bend kick with toes

5.后点步冲拳 hòu diǎn bù chōng quán
back leg toe point on floor and punch

6.歇步挑掌 xiē bù tiāo zhǎng
cross leg stance and flick palm upward

7.并步冲拳 bìng bù chōng quán
close feet and punch forward

8.腾空摆莲 360° téng kōng bǎi lián 360°
lotus jump kick 360°

9.并步拍地 bìng bù pāi dì
slam ground with feet together

10.单拍脚 dān pāi jiǎo
front slap kick

11.提膝跳冲拳 tí xī tiào chōng quán
jump with raised knee and punch

12.腾空飞脚 téng kōng fēi jiǎo
front slap jump kick

13.侧空翻 cè kōng fān
aerial

14.旋风脚 360° xuán fēng jiǎo 360°
tornado jump kick 360°

15.跌竖叉 diē shù chā
split

第二段　　　　　　　Part 2
16.盖步冲拳 gài bù chōng quán
cover step and punch

17.单拍脚 dān pāi jiǎo
front slap kick

18.侧踹腿 cè chuài tuǐ
bend side kick

19.抡臂拍地 lūn bì pāi dì
wheel arms into downward slam

20.震脚按掌 zhèn jiǎo àn zhǎng
stomp and downward press

21.弓步冲拳 gōng bù chōng quán
bow stance punch

22.横档步亮掌 héng dàng bù liàng zhǎng
sideways bow stance with hook and palm

23.踢腿撩掌 tī tuǐ liāo zhǎng
straight kick and circle palm toward body

24.跳提膝勾手推掌 tiào tí xī gōu shǒu tuī zhǎng
raised knee jump with pushing palm and hook

25.腾空箭弹 téng kōng jiàn dàn
jump bend kick

26.叉步双摆掌 chā bù shuāng bǎi zhǎng
cross leg steps and circle block with both palms

27.弓步勾手推掌 gōng bù gōu shǒu tuī zhǎng
bow staance with hook and push palm

28.挑转身仆步切掌 tiāo zhuǎn shēn pū bù qiē zhǎng
turn and jump into crouch stance with chopping palm

29.弓步架冲拳 gōng bù jià chōng quán
bow stance with upper block and forward punch

149

30.弓步贯拳 gōng bù guàn quán
bow stance and swing fist sideways

31.后扫腿 hòu sǎo tuǐ
backward sweep

32.仆步亮掌 pū bù liàng zhǎng
crouch stance with hook and palm

第三段   **Part 3**

33.正踢腿 zhèng tī tuǐ
straight kick

34.燕式平衡 yàn shì píng héng
swallow style balance

35.弓步十字拳 gōng bù shí zì quán
bow stance and punch fists perpendicularly to stance

36.弓步左冲拳 gōng bù zuǒ chōng quán
bow stance and left punch

37.提膝挑掌 tí xī tiāo zhǎng
raise knee and flip palm upward

38.弧形步 hú xíng bù
crescent steps

39.扣腿双摆掌 kòu tuǐ shuāng bǎi zhǎng
pin leg and circle both arms

40.击步劈打 jī bù pī dǎ
gallop and chop hit

41.弓步靠掌 gōng bù kào zhǎng
bow stance with open palms

42.弓步双勾手 gōng bù shuāng gōu shǒu
bow stance with both hands hook

43.垫步蹬腿 diàn bù dēng tuǐ
skip into bend kick with heel

44.弓步劈拳 gōng bù pī quán
bow stance and fist chop

45.马步托打 mǎ bù tuō dǎ
horse stance with drag and punch

46.插步抓肩 chā bù zhuā jiān
cross leg step and grab shoulder

47.马步架打 mǎ bù jià dǎ
horse stance punch with upper block

第四段   **Part 4**
48.提膝架掌 tí xī jià zhǎng
raise knee and block with palms

49.提膝冲拳 tí xī chōng quán
raise knee and punch

50.旋子 xuán zǐ
butterfly jump

51.坐盘 zuò pán
cross leg sit

52.外摆腿击响 wài bǎi tuǐ jī xiǎng
slapping outside kick

53.打虎式 dǎ hǔ shì
hit the tiger pose

54.弓步顶肘 gōng bù dǐng zhǒu
bow stance and hit with elbow

55.抡臂砸拳 lūn bì zá quán
circle arms and smash fist

56.虚步挑掌 xū bù tiāo zhǎng
empty stance and flick palm upward

57.转身云手 zhuǎn shēn yún shǒu
turn around and circle block with palms above head

58.并步摆拳 bìng bù bǎi quán
feet together and hold fist

收势 shōu shì
closing form

A Group Jianshu (Straightsword) Form
A组剑术竞赛套路

预备势 yù bèi shì
preparation stance

第一段   **Part 1**
1.并步持剑 bìng bù chí jiàn
feet together and hold sword

2.云剑 yún jiàn
circle sword above head

3.上步侧踢腿 shàng bù cè tī tuǐ
step forward and bend side kick

4.虚步扣剑 xū bù kòu jiàn
empty stance and hold sword inward

5.退步反撩剑 tuì bù fǎn liāo jiàn
step back and flick sword backward

6.剪腕花 jiǎn wàn huā
figure eight sword with wrist

7.转身背花 zhuǎn shēn bèi huā
turn around and circle sword behind back

8.剪腕花 jiǎn wàn huā
figure eight sword with wrist

9.弓步刺剑 gōng bù cì jiàn
bow stance and sword thrust

10.背花 bèi huā
circle sword with wrist behind back

11.剪腕花 jiǎn wàn huā
figure eight sword with wrist

12.提膝上刺剑 tí xī shàng cì jiàn
raise knee and sword thrust upward

13.剪腕花 jiǎn wàn huā
figure eight sword with wrist

14.挂剑 guà jiàn
circle hook sword

15.提膝崩剑 tí xī bēng jiàn
raise knee and flick sword

16.弧形步 hú xíng bù
crescent steps

17.跳提膝平斩剑 tiào tí xī píng zhǎn jiàn
raised knee jump with horizontal sword hit

18.上步刺剑 shàng bù cì jiàn
step forward and thrust sword

19.翻身扫剑 fān shēn sǎo jiàn
rotate body and sweep sword

20.击步点剑 jī bù diǎn jiàn
gallop and point sword downward

21.旋风脚360° xuán fēng jiǎo 360°
tornade jump kick 360°

22.跌竖叉 diē shù chā
split

第二段   **Part 2**
23.剪腕花 jiǎn wàn huā
figure eight sword with wrist

24.反挂剑 fǎn guà jiàn
hook sword in a backward circle

25.丁步前点剑 dīng bù qián diǎn jiàn
point sword forward into t-step

26.插步反穿剑 chā bù fǎn chuān jiàn
cross leg step and pierce sword backward

27.剪腕花 jiǎn wàn huā
figure eight sword with wrist

28.背花 bèi huā
circle sword with wrist behind back

29.下劈剑 xià pī jiàn
chop sword downward

30.提膝刺剑 tí xī cì jiàn
raise knee and thrust sword

31.换跳步交接剑 huàn tiào bù jiāo jiē jiàn
jump step and switch sword to other hand

32.转身云剑 zhuǎn shēn yún jiàn
turn around and circle sword above head

33.旋子 xuán zǐ
butterfly jump

34.交接剑 jiāo jiē jiàn
switch sword to other hand

35.转身云剑 zhuǎn shēn yún jiàn
turn around and circle sword above head

36.坐盘 zuò pán
cross leg sit

37.转身云剑 zhuǎn shēn yún jiàn
turn around and circle sword above head

38.望月平衡 wàng yuè píng héng
crescent back balance

第三段   Part 3
39.上步撩剑 shàng bù liāo jiàn
step foward and upper circle with sword

40.退步反撩剑 tuì bù fǎn liāo jiàn
step back and circle block upward with sword

41.转身腕花 zhuǎn shēn wàn huā
turn around and circle sword with wrist

42.跪步下截剑 guì bù xià jié jiàn
kneeling stance and diagonal sword chop

43.剪腕花 jiǎn wàn huā
figure eight sword with wrist

44.扣步云剑 kòu bù yún jiàn
pin leg and circle sword above head

45.弧形步抹剑 hú xíng bù mǒ jiàn
crescent steps and slide sword

46.跳提膝反撩剑 tiào tí xī fǎn liāo jiàn
raised knee jump and upward circle block with sword

47.剪腕花 jiǎn wàn huā
figure eight sword with wrist

48.插步平斩剑 chā bù píng zhǎn jiàn
cross leg and horizontally hit with sword

49.转身云剑 zhuǎn shēn yún jiàn
turn around and circle sword above head

50.退步刺剑 tuì bù cì jiàn
step back and thrust sword

51.撤步穿剑 chè bù chuān jiàn
step and pierce sword

52.剪腕花 jiǎn wàn huā
figure eight sword with wrist

53.提膝点剑 tí xī diǎn jiàn
raise knee and point sword

54.跳崩剑 tiào bēng jiàn
jump and flick sword upward

55.仆步带剑 pū bù dài jiàn
crouch stance and upper block with sword

第四段   **Part 4**
56.并步下截剑 bìng bù xià jié jiàn
feet together and diagonally hit sword downward

57.左右挂剑 zuǒ yòu guà jiàn
hook sword in a circle on left and right sides

58.背后穿挂剑 bèi hòu chuān guà jiàn
pierce sword behind back into circle hook

59. 跳换步抛接剑 tiào huàn bù pāo jiē jiàn
jump step and toss sword into other hand

60.侧空翻 cè kōng fān
aerial
61.上步拍脚 shàng bù pāi jiǎo
step forward and front slap kick

62.弓步持剑 gōng bù chí jiàn
bow stance and hold sword

63.并步持剑上指 bìng bù chí jiàn shàng zhǐ
close feet with sword finger pointing upward
and hold sword

收势shōu shì
closing form

A Group Daoshu (Broadsword) Form
A组刀术竞赛套路

预备势 yù bèi shì
preparation stance

第一段   **Part 1**

1.并步抱刀冲拳 bìng bù bào dāo chōng quán
close feet with punch and hold broadsword

2.接刀退步腕花 jiē dāo tuì bù wàn huā
switch broadsword onto other hand and step back with
broadsword circle around wrist

3.后点步持刀推掌 hòu diǎn bù chí dāo tuī zhǎng
hold broadsword and push palm with back leg toe
point on floor

4.上步扣腿扎刀 shàng bù kòu tuǐ zā dāo
step forward into broadsword thrust and pin leg

5.缠头刀 chán tóu dāo
twine broadsword around head from front

159

6.转身裹脑刀 zhuǎn shēn guǒ nǎo dāo
turn around and wrap broadsword around head
from back

7.弓步藏刀推掌 gōng bù cáng dāo tuī zhǎng
hide the broadsword and push palm with bow stance

8.右左平扎刀 yòu zuǒ píng zā dāo
thrust broadsword at shoulder level on right
and left sides

9.转身背花扎刀 zhuǎn shēn bèi huā zā dāo
turn around and circle broadsword with wrist behind
back into broadsword thrust

10.并步拍地 bìng bù pāi dì
close feet and slam on ground

11.跳起提膝扎刀 tiào qǐ tí xī zā dāo
raised knee jump with broadsword thrust

12.击步抱刀 jī bù bào dāo
gallop and hold broadsword

13.腾空飞脚 téng kōng fēi jiǎo
front slap jump kick

14.侧空翻 cè kōng fān
aerial

15.腾空旋风脚 360° téng kōng xuán fēng jiǎo 360°
tornado jump kick 360°

16.跌竖叉 diē shù chā
split

第二段   **Part 2**

17.后点步带刀 hòu diǎn bù dài dāo
back leg toe point on ground and retract broadsword

18.剪腕花转身扎刀 jiǎn wàn huā zhuǎn shēn zā dāo
figure eight broadsword with wrist and turn around
into broadsword thrust

19.转身缠头刀 zhuǎn shēn chán tóu dāo
turn around and twine broadsword around head
from front

20.转身裹脑刀 zhuǎn shēn guǒ nǎo dāo
turn around and wrap broadsword around head
from back

21.斜拍脚扎刀 xié pāi jiǎo zā dāo
diagonal slap kick and thrust

22.腾空摆莲 360° 接马步
téng kōng bǎi lián 360° jiē mǎ bù
lotus jump kick 360° into horse stance

23.退步云刀 tuì bù yún dāo
cirlce block broadsword above head and step back

24.换跳步扎刀 huàn tiào bù zā dāo
switch legs jump with broadsword thrust

25.侧身云刀 cè shēn yún dāo
sideways circle block with broadsword

26.平扎刀 píng zā dāo
thrust broadsword at shoulder level

27.背花刀 bèi huā dāo
circle broadsword with wrist behind back

28.倒插步缠头刀 dǎo chā bù chán tóu dāo
backward cross step and twine broadsword
around head from front

29.前扫腿扫刀 qián sǎo tuǐ sǎo dāo
forward sweep and sweep broadsword

30.上步扎刀 shàng bù zā dāo
step forward and thrust broadsword

31.腾空回身扫刀 téng kōng huí shēn sǎo dāo
jump and turn to sweep broadsword backward

32.转身缠头裹脑刀 zhuǎn shēn chán tóu guǒ nǎo dāo
turn around into broadsword wrap around head
from the front and back

33.弓步云刀 gōng bù yún dāo
bow stance and sideways circle block with broadsword

34.换跳步弓步扎刀 huàn tiào bù gōng bù zā dāo
jump and switch legs into bow stance thrust

第三段   Part 3
35.转身挂撩刀 zhuǎn shēn guà liāo dāo
turn around into broadsword circle hook and
upward circle block

36.斩刀 zhǎn dāo
horizontal broadsword cut

37.转身 zhuǎn shēn
turn around

38.挑起提膝斩刀 tiāo qǐ tí xī zhǎn dāo
raised knee jump and horizontally cut broadsword

39.旋子扫刀 xuán zǐ sǎo dāo
butterfly jump and sweep broadsword

40.坐盘抱刀 zuò pán bào dāo
cross leg sit and hold broadsword

41.转身裹脑抡劈刀 zhuǎn shēn guǒ nǎo lūn pī dāo
turn around and wrap broadsword around head
from back into swinging chop

42.盖步翻身抡劈刀 gài bù fān shēn lūn pī dāo
cover step and turn around with swinging
broadsword chop

43.回身蹬脚扎刀 huí shēn dēng jiǎo zā dāo
turn around into bend kick with heel and
broadsword thrust

44.弓步带刀 gōng bù dài dāo
bow stance and retract broadsword

第四段   **Part 4**
45.并步下扎 bìng bù xià zā
thrust broadsword downward with feet together

46.转身撞步绞刀 zhuǎn shēn zhuàng bù jiǎo dāo
turn around and circle broadsword with stomp steps

47.平推刀 píng tuī dāo
push horizontal broadsword forward

48. 转身下截刀 zhuǎn shēn xià jié dāo
turn around and diagonally hit broadsword downward

49.转身并步斜扎 zhuǎn shēn bìng bù xié zā
turn around and broadsword thrust diagonally
upward with feet together

163

50.仆步持刀 pū bù chí dāo
crouch stance and hold broadsword

51.扎刀 zā dāo
thrust broadsword

52.转身接刀 zhuǎn shēn jiē dāo
turn around and switch broadsword onto other hand

53.虚步反持刀 xū bù fǎn chí dāo
empty stance and hold broadsword backward

54.持刀按掌 chí dāo àn zhǎng
hold broad sword and press palms downward

收势 shōu shì
closing form

A Group Gunshu (Staff) Form
A组棍术竞赛套路

预备势 yù bèi shì
preparation form

第一段   **Part 1**
1.并步推棍 bìng bù tuī gùn
feet together and push vertical staff forward

2.转身抡棍 zhuǎn shēn lūn gùn
turn around and swing staff

3.弓步背棍盘肘 gōng bù bèi gùn pán zhǒu
bow stance with elbow block and hold staff
behind back

4.云棍 yún gùn
circle block with staff above head

5.撤步绞棍 chè bù jiǎo gùn
step back and circle staff base

6.转身抡棍 zhuǎn shēn lūn gùn
turn around and swing staff

7.仆步摔棍 pū bù shuāi gùn
crouch stance and slam staff

8.转身摔棍 zhuǎn shēn shuāi gùn
turn around and slam staff

9.左右点棍 zuǒ yòu diǎn gùn
point staff to the left and right

10.单手平抡棍 dān shǒu píng lūn gùn
swing staff horizontally with one hand

11.腾空背棍提膝冲拳
téng kōng bèi gùn tí xī chōng quán
raised knee jump with forward punch and staff
behind back

12.腾空飞脚 téng kōng fēi jiǎo
front slap jump kick

13. 侧空翻 cè kōng fān
aerial

14.旋风脚 360° xuán fēng jiǎo 360°
tornado jump kick 360°

15.跌竖叉 diē shù chā
split

第二段　　　　　　　Part 2
16.转身抡棍 zhuǎn shēn lūn gùn
turn around and swing staff

17.弓步拨棍 gōng bù bō gùn
circle staff above head into bow stance

18.涮腰抡棍 shuàn yāo lūn gùn
pivot body around waist and swing staff

19.背棍斜拍脚 bèi gùn xié pāi jiǎo
diagonal front slap kick with staff behind back

20.腾空摆莲 360° téng kōng bǎi lián 360°
lotus jump kick 360°

21.弓步拨把 gōng bù bō bǎ
bow stance and swing staff base

22.仆步摔棍 pū bù shuāi gùn
crouch stance and slam staff

23.点棍 diǎn gùn
point staff

24.转身提撩棍 zhuǎn shēn tí liāo gùn
turn and circle block with staff upward

25.仆步摔棍 pū bù shuāi gùn
crouch stance and slam staff

26.左右点棍 zuǒ yòu diǎn gùn
point staff to left and right

27.扫棍 sǎo gùn
sweep staff

28.抡棍 lūn gùn
swing staff

29. 点棍盖把 diǎn gùn gài bǎ
point staff and downward hit with staff base

30. 抡棍 lūn gùn
swing staff

31. 翻身仆步摔棍 fān shēn pū bù shuāi gùn
rotate body into crouch stance and slam staff

32. 抡棍弓步推掌 lūn gùn gōng bù tuī zhǎng
swing staff into bow stance and push palm

第三段   Part 3
33. 上步转身抡棍 shàng bù zhuǎn shēn lūn gùn
step forward and turn while swinging staff

34. 抡棍平扫 lūn gùn píng sǎo
swing staff and sweep staff horizontally

35. 旋子扫棍 xuán zǐ sǎo gùn
butteryfly jump and sweep staff

36. 坐盘抡棍 zuò pán lūn gùn
swing staff into cross leg sit

37. 转身抡棍 zhuǎn shēn lūn gùn
turn around and swing staff

38. 舞花背棍 wǔ huā bèi gùn
circle block downward on both sides and circle staff
behind back

39. 盖步戳把 gài bù chuō bǎ
cover step and hit with staff base

40. 抡棍仆步抱棍 lūn gùn pū bù bào gùn
swing staff into coruch stance and hold staff

41.舞花提撩棍 wǔ huā tí liāo gùn
circle block downward on both sides into circle
block upward on both sides

42.撤步劈 chè bù pī gùn
step backward and staff chop

43.转身抡棍 zhuǎn shēn lūn gùn
turn around and swing staff

44.提膝跳背棍 tí xī tiào bèi gùn
raised knee jump and hold staff behind back

45.舞花仆步摔棍 wǔ huā pū bù shuāi gùn
circle block downward on both sides into crouch
stance and slam staff

46.并步崩棍 bìng bù bēng gùn
feet together and flick staff head upward

47.单手抡棍 dān shǒu lūn gùn
swing staff with one hand

48.背棍虚步推掌 bèi gùn xū bù tuī zhǎng
empty stance with staff behind back and push palm

49.弓步拨棍 gōng bù bō gùn
bow stance block with staff base

50.并步持棍 bìng bù chí gùn
close feet and hold staff

收势 shōu shì
closing form

A Group Qiangshu (Spear) Form
A组枪术竞赛套路

预备势 yù bèi shì
preparation form

第一段   **Part 1**

1.虚步架枪 xū bù jià qiāng
empty stance and upper block with spear

2.抱枪侧踢腿 bào qiāng cè tī tuǐ
hold spear and side kick

3.跃步劈枪 yuè bù pī qiāng
jump and spear chop

4.弓步扎枪 gōng bù zā qiāng
bow stance and spear thrust

5.弓步拦拿扎枪 (4个) gōng bù lán ná zā qiāng（4 gè）
bow stance with outer and inner blocks into spear
thrust (4 times)

6.提膝下拨枪 tí xī xià bō qiāng
raise knee and lower spear block

7.插步拨枪 (2个) chā bù bō qiāng (2 gè)
cross leg steps and spear block

8.跳插步下扎枪 tiào chā bù xià zā qiāng
jump into cross leg stance and spear thrust downward

9.弧形步 hú xíng bù
crescent steps

10.跨步劈枪 kuà bù pī qiāng
leap step and chop spear

11.跳步架枪 tiào bù jià qiāng
jump step and upper spear block

12.旋风脚 360° xuán fēng jiǎo 360°
tornado jump kick 360°

13.跌竖叉 diē shù chā
split

第二段   **Part 2**
14.并步托枪 bìng bù tuō qiāng
feet together with spear above head

15.半蹲缠枪 bàn dūn chán qiāng
feet together with slight bend and rotate spear base

16.回身劈枪 huí shēn pī qiāng
turn around and spear chop

17.跳转劈枪 tiào zhuǎn pī qiāng
turn and jump into spear chop

18.反身云绞枪 fǎn shēn yún jiǎo qiāng
rotate body and circle block above head with spear and
rotate spear base

19.前点步斜下横崩枪
qián diǎn bù xié xià héng bēng qiāng
high empty stance and flip spear head
diagonally downward

20.抛接枪 pāo jiē qiāng
throw and catch spear

21.击步反扎枪 jī bù fǎn zā qiāng
gallop and spear thrust with right palm down

22.舞花过背枪 wǔ huā guò bèi qiāng
circle spear block on both sides and then circle spear
around back

23.腾空摆莲 360° téng kōng bǎi lián 360°
lotus jump kick 360°

24.弓步云拨枪 gōng bù yún bō qiāng
circle block above head into bow stance with spear hit

25.转身云枪 zhuǎn shēn yún qiāng
turn around and circle block spear above head

26.弧形步绞枪 hú xíng bù jiǎo qiāng
crescent steps and rotate spear base

27.转身横击把 zhuǎn shēn héng jī bǎ
turn around and hit with spear base

28.上步拦扎枪 shàng bù lán zā qiāng
step forward with outer and inner blocks into
spear thrust

29.腾空箭弹崩枪 téng kōng jiàn dàn bēng qiāng
jump bend kick and flip spear head upward

30.并步挑把 bìng bù tiāo bǎ
feet together and flip staff base upward

31.弓步拦拿扎枪 gōng bù lán ná zā qiāng
bow stance with outer and inner blocks into spear
thrust

32.绞劈枪 jiǎo pī qiāng
rotate spear base and spear chop

33.扣腿点枪 kòu tuǐ diǎn qiāng
pin leg and point spear downward

34.弓步崩枪 gōng bù bēng qiāng
bow stance and flip spear head upward

第三段   Part 3
35.挑把翻身挑枪 tiāo bǎ fān shēn tiāo qiāng
block spear base upward into turn around and
block spear head upward

36.盖跳步拦拿扎枪 gài tiào bù lán ná zā qiāng
front cross step hop with outer and inner blocks
into spear thrust

37.转身单手扎枪 zhuǎn shēn dān shǒu zā qiāng
turn around and spear thrust with one hand

38.上步背穿接枪 shàng bù bèi chuān jiē qiāng
step forward with spear pierce behind back and
catch spear

39.腾空跳架枪 téng kōng tiào jià qiāng
jump and spear block aboe head

40.仆步摔枪 pū bù shuāi qiāng
crouch stance and spear slam

41.反身跳戳把 fǎn shēn tiào chuō bǎ
jump and turn into hit with spear base

42.舞花过背枪 wǔ huā guò bèi qiāng
circle spear block on both sides and then circle
spear around back

43.坐盘下扎枪 zuò pán xià zā qiāng
cross leg sit and spear thrust downward

第四段　　　　　　　　　Part 4
44.回身劈枪 huí shēn pī qiāng
turn around and spear chop

45.跳提膝架枪 tiào tí xī jià qiāng
raised knee jump and hold spear above head

46.跳换步下扎枪 tiào huàn bù xià zā qiāng
switch legs jump and spear thrust downward

47.上步侧空翻 shàng bù cè kōng fān
step forward and aerial

48.上步正踢腿 shàng bù zhèng tī tuǐ
step forward and straight kick

49.仆步背拖枪 pū bù bèi tuō qiāng
crouch stance and pull the spear behind back

50.弓步拦拿扎枪 gōng bù lán ná zā qiāng
bow stance with outer and inner blocks into
spear thrust

51.弓步扫把 gōng bù sǎo bǎ
bow stance sweep spear base

52.丁步握枪按掌 dīng bù wò qiāng àn zhǎng
hold spear and press palm with t-step

53.并步立枪推掌 bìng bù lì qiāng tuī zhǎng
hold spear vertically and push palm with feet together

收势 shōu shì
closing form

A Group Nanquan (South-
ern Style Barehand) Form
A组南拳竞赛套路

预备式 yù bèi shì
preparation form

第一段　　　　　　　**Part 1**
1.并步抱拳 bìng bù bào quán
feet together and hold fists

2.震脚抱拳 zhèn jiǎo bào quán
stomp and hold fists

3.半马步按掌 bàn mǎ bù àn zhǎng
shifted horse stance and press palms

4.右拍脚 yòu pāi jiǎo
right front slap kick

5.单蝶步截桥（发声：嘿）
dān dié bù jié qiáo (fā shēng: hēi)
single butterfly stance and block with forearm
(shout: hey)

6.马步双挑掌伏掌 mǎ bù shuāng tiāo zhǎng fú zhǎng
horse stance and flip both palms up into downward
press in front

7.马步双穿桥 mǎ bù shuāng chuān qiáo
horse stance and twisting pierce with both forearms

8.马步托掌沉桥 mǎ bù tuō zhǎng chén qiáo
lift palms and sink forearm with horse stance

9.马步双推单指 mǎ bù shuāng tuī dān zhǐ
horse stance and push point palm with both hands

10.马步双标掌沉桥
mǎ bù shuāng biāo zhǎng chén qiáo
horse stance and thrust both palms vertically with
fingers forward and sink forearms

11.独立步反撩爪 dú lì bù fǎn liāo zhǎo
stand on one leg and backward block with tiger claw

12.换跳步抓面爪 huàn tiào bù zhuā miàn zhǎo
switch legs jump and scratch with tiger claw

13.旋风脚 360° xuán fēng jiǎo 360°
tornado jump kick 360°

14.单蝶步虎爪 dān dié bù hǔ zhǎo
single butterfly stance and tiger claw push

15.横钉腿按掌 héng dīng tuǐ àn zhǎng
diagonal nail kick and press palm

16.腾空外摆腿 450° téng kōng wài bǎi tuǐ 450°
jump outside kick 450°

17.马步交叉手 mǎ bù jiāo chā shǒu
horse stance and cross hands

第二段 Part 2
18.弓步挂盖拳 gōng bù guà gài quán
bowstance and downward swinging block hit

19.插步鞭拳 chā bù biān quán
cross step and whip fist

20.弓步挂盖拳 gōng bù guà gài quán
bowstance and downward swinging block hit

21.退步冲拳 tuì bù chōng quán
step back and punch

22.横踩腿拨掌 héng cǎi tuǐ bō zhǎng
low diagonal heel kick and retract palms

23.骑龙步横切掌 qí lóng bù héng qiē zhǎng
dragon-riding stance and chop palms horizontall

24.弓步抛拳 (发声: 嘿)
gōng bù pāo quán (fā shēng: hēi)
fist swing upward into bow stance (shout: hey)

25.上步连环抛拳 shàng bù lián huán pāo quán
forward steps with consecutive upward fist
swings on both arms

26.弓步抛拳 gōng bù pāo quán
fist swing upward into bow stance

27.侧踹腿劈拳 cè chuài tuǐ pī quán
bend side kick and chop with fists

28.弓步挂盖拳 gōng bù guà gài quán
bowstance and downward swinging block hit

29.弓步左右双鞭拳
gōng bù zuǒ yòu shuāng biān quán
bow stance and whip both fists

30.上步左右劈拳 shàng bù zuǒ yòu pī quán
step forward with fist chop on both sides

31.骑龙步左右挂拳 qí lóng bù zuǒ yòu guà quán
hook fist on both sides with dragon-riding stance

32.震脚双挂拳 zhèn jiǎo shuāng guà quán
stomp and hit back of both fist downward

33.弓步单指（发声：的）
gōng bù dān zhǐ （fā shēng: de）
bow stance with pointer palm forward (shout: de)

34.旋风脚360° xuán fēng jiǎo 360°
tornado jump kick 360°

35.单蝶步截桥 dān dié bù jié qiáo
single butterfly step and block with forearm

36.高虚步蛇形手 gāo xū bù shé xíng shǒu
high empty stance with snake hands

37.腾空外摆腿360° téng kōng wài bǎi tuǐ 360°
lotus jump kick 360°

38.马步截桥 mǎ bù jié qiáo
horse stance and block with forearm

179

39.弓步双推单指 gōng bù shuāng tuī dān zhǐ
bow stance and push with both pointer palms

40.弓步标掌沉桥 gōng bù biāo zhǎng chén qiáo
bow stance and thrust both palms vertically with fingers forward and sink forearms

41.弓步挂盖拳 gōng bù guà gài quán
bowstance and downward swinging block hit

42.马步抛撞拳 mǎ bù pāo zhuàng quán
horse stance and uppercut fist

43.盖步截桥 gài bù jié qiáo
front cover step and forearm block

44.马步鞭拳 mǎ bù biān quán
horse stance and whip fist

45.半马步双弹拳（发声：嗌）
bàn mǎ bù shuāng dàn quán （fā shēng: yì）
shifted horse stance and hit back of both fists forward
(shout: yi)

46.半马步连环冲拳 bàn mǎ bù lián huán chōng quán
shifted horse stance with consecutive punches

47.马步顶肘 mǎ bù dǐng zhǒu
horse stance and hit with elbow

48.高虚步鹤嘴手 gāo xū bù hè zuǐ shǒu
high empty stance with crane beak hands

49.弓步虎爪（发声：哇）
gōng bù hǔ zhǎo （fā shēng: wā）
bow stance with tiger claws (shout: wa)

50.独立步虎爪 dú lì bù hǔ zhǎo
stand on one leg and tiger claws

51.腾空盘腿 360°侧扑 téng kōng pán tuǐ 360° cè pū
turning leg swing jump 360° into sideways laying

52.剪扫侧踹腿 jiǎn sǎo cè chuài tuǐ
scissor kick legs into upward kick

53.鲤鱼打挺 lǐ yú dǎ tǐng
kick up

54.骑龙步抛撞拳 qí lóng bù pāo zhuàng quán
dragon-riding stance with swinging uppercut

55.弓步滚桥 gōng bù gǔn qiáo
bow stance with twisted forearm block

第四段   **Part 4**
56.上步勒手 shàng bù lè shǒu
step forward and grab

57.跟步双插掌 gēn bù shuāng chā zhǎng
forward steps and thrust both palms with
fingers forward

58.跟步双切掌 gēn bù shuāng qiē zhǎng
forward steps and chop with both palms

59. 托步双托掌 tuō bù shuāng tuō zhǎng
step and drag back leg forward with both palms lift

60.弓步劈挂拳（发声：嘿）
gōng bù pī guà quán （fā shēng: hēi)
bow stance and hook fist into chop (shout: hey)

61.虚步推掌冲拳 xū bù tuī zhǎng chōng quán
empty stance with push palm and punch

62.并步抱拳 bìng bù bào quán
close feet and hold fists

收势 shōu shì
closing form

A Group Nandao (Southern Style Broadsword) Form
A组南刀竞赛套路

预备势 yù bèi shì
preparation form

第一段   **Part 1**
1.马步按刀 mǎ bù àn dāo
horse stance and press Nandao

2.震脚藏刀 zhèn jiǎo cáng dāo
stomp and hide Nandao

3.麒麟步弓步推刀（发声: 嘿）
qí lín bù gōng bù tuī dāo (fā shēng: hēi)
Qilin steps into bow stance and push Nandao
(shout: hey)

4.转身半马步扎刀 zhuǎn shēn bàn mǎ bù zā dāo
turn around into shifted horse stance and
Nandao thrust

5.骑龙步崩刀 qí lóng bù bēng dāo
dragon-riding stance and flick Nandao upward

6.上步砍刀 shàng bù kǎn dāo
step forward with Nandao hack

7.半马步砍刀（发声：嘿）
bàn mǎ bù kǎn dāo (fā shēng: hēi)
shifted horse stance with Nandao hack (shout: hey)

8.盖步截刀 gài bù jié dāo
cover step and switch Nandao onto other hand

9.骑龙步扎刀 qí lóng bù zā dāo
dragon-riding stance with Nandao thrust

10.上步旋风脚 450° shàng bù xuán fēng jiǎo 450°
step forward and tornado jump kick 450°

11.单蝶步按刀 dān dié bù àn dāo
single butterfly step and Nandao press

12.高虚步撞柄 gāo xū bù zhuàng bǐng
high empty stance and hit with Nandao handle

13.上步腾空外摆腿 360°
shàng bù téng kōng wài bǎi tuǐ 360°
step forward and lotus jump kick 360°

14.马步反握刀 mǎ bù fǎn wò dāo
horse stance and hold Nandao backward

15.插步反扎刀 chā bù fǎn zā dāo
cross leg steps and thrust Nandao in direction of elbow

16.退步左右抹刀 tuì bù zuǒ yòu mǒ dāo
step back with Nandao slide on both sides

17.马步反扎刀 mǎ bù fǎn zā dāo
shifted horsestance and thrust Nandao in
direction of elbow

18.跳单拍脚插步反扎刀
tiào dān pāi jiǎo chā bù fǎn zā dāo
jump with front slap kick into cross step back and
thrust Nandao in direction of elbow

19.弓步抹刀 gōng bù mǒ dāo
bow stance with Nandao slide

第二段　　　　　　　Part 2
20.骑龙步反撩刀 qí lóng bù fǎn liāo dāo
dragon-riding stance and circle block Nandao upward

21.骑龙步砍刀 qí lóng bù kǎn dāo
dragon-riding stance with Nandao hack

22.转身反撩刀 zhuǎn shēn fǎn liāo dāo
turn around and circle block Nandao upward

23.退步左右扫刀 tuì bù zuǒ yòu sǎo dāo
step back with Nandao sweep on left and right sides

24.跳转身骑龙步砍刀（发声: 嘿）
tiào zhuǎn shēn qí lóng bù kǎn dāo (fā shēng: hēi)
jump and turn into dragon-riding stance with Nandao
hack (shout: hey)

25.弓步带刀 gōng bù dài dāo
bow stance and retract Nandao

26.盖步缠头劈刀 gài bù chán tóu pī dāo
cover step and twine Nandao around head from
front into chop

185

27.垫步马步劈刀 diàn bù mǎ bù pī dāo
hop into horse stance with Nandao chop

28.转身右劈刀 zhuǎn shēn yòu pī dāo
turn around into right Nandao chop

29.马步劈刀 mǎ bù pī dāo
horse stance with Nandao chop

30.跳转身马步砍刀 tiào zhuǎn shēn mǎ bù kǎn dāo
jump and turn into horse stance with Nandao hack

31.独立步捧刀 dú lì bù pěng dāo
stand on one leg and hold Nandao

32.上步旋风脚360° shàng bù xuán fēng jiǎo 360°
step forward and tornade jump kick 360°

33.上步扎刀 shàng bù zā dāo
step forward and Nandao thrust

34.腾空外摆腿450° téng kōng wài bǎi tuǐ 450°
lotus jump kick 450°

35.马步砍刀 mǎ bù kǎn dāo
horse stance with Nandao hack

36.退步腕花刀单推指 tuì bù wàn huā dāo dān tuī zhǐ
step back with figure eight Nandao and pointer
palm push

37.剪腕花翻身跳砍刀
jiǎn wàn huā fān shēn tiào kǎn dāo
figure eight Nandao and jump turn into Nandao hack

186

38.翻身跳砍刀 fān shēn tiào kǎn dāo
turn and jump into Nandao hack

39.单蝶步砍刀 dān dié bù kǎn dāo
single butterfly stance with Nandao hack

40.上步剪腕花刀 shàng bù jiǎn wàn huā dāo
step forward and figure eight Nandao

41.马步推刀虎爪（发声：嗌）
mǎ bù tuī dāo hǔ zhǎo (fā shēng: yì)
horse stance with Nandao push and tiger claw
(shout: yi)

第三段   **Part 3**
42.左右骑龙步砍刀 zuǒ yòu qí lóng bù kǎn dāo
dragon-riding stance with Nandao hack on left
and right sides

43.裹脑刀震脚截刀 guǒ nǎo dāo zhèn jiǎo jié dāo
wrap Nandao around head from back and stop
with Nandao block

44.麒麟步弓步扎刀（发声：嗌）
qí lín bù gōng bù zā dāo(fā shēng: yì)
Qilin steps into bow stance with Nandao thrust
(shout: yi)

45.独立步挫刀 dú lì bù cuò dāo
stand on one leg with Nandao forward block

46.上步腾空盘腿360°侧扑
shàng bù téng kōng pán tuǐ 360° cè pū
step forward and turning leg swing jump 360°
into sideways laying

47.鲤鱼打挺 lǐ yú dǎ tǐng
kick up

48.上步左右格刀 shàng bù zuǒ yòu gé dāo
step forward with Nandao block on left and righ sides

49.骑龙步截刀 qí lóng bù jié dāo
dragon-riding stance with Nandao forward block

50.麒麟步弓步推刀 qí lín bù gōng bù tuī dāo
Qilin steps into bow stance and Nandao push

第四段   **Part 4**
51.上步左右砍刀 shàng bù zuǒ yòu kǎn dāo
step forward with Nandao hack on left and right sides

52.上步剪腕花刀 shàng bù jiǎn wàn huā dāo
step forward and figure eight Nandao

53.垫步弹踢点刀 diàn bù dàn tī diǎn dāo
hop into bend kick with toe and Nandao point

54.上步勾踢崩刀 shàng bù gōu tī bēng dāo
step forward with hook kick and flick Nandao upward

55.上步左右劈刀 shàng bù zuǒ yòu pī dāo
step forward with Nandao chop on left and right sides

56.半马步砍刀 bàn mǎ bù kǎn dāo
shifted horse stance with Nandao hack

57.骑龙步扎刀 qí lóng bù zā dāo
dragon-riding stance with Nandao thrust

58.盖步砍刀 gài bù kǎn dāo
cover step with Nandao hack

59.虚步崩刀 xū bù bēng dāo
empty stance and flick Nandao

60.麒麟步跪步推刀（发声：嘿）
qí lín bù guì bù tuī dāo（fā shēng: hēi)
Qilin steps into kneeling stance with Nandao push
(shout: hey)

61.半马步捧刀 bàn mǎ bù pěng dāo
shifted horse stance and hold Nandao

62.并步反握刀柄 bìng bù fǎn wò dāo bǐng
feet together and hold Nandao behind arm

收势 shōu shì
closing form

A Group Nangun (Southern Style Staff) Form
A组南棍竞赛套路

预备势 yù bèi shì
preparation form

第一段　　　　　　**Part 1**
1.并步推棍 bìng bù tuī gùn
push Nangun with feet together

2.马步挂劈棍（发声：嘿）
mǎ bù guà pī gùn (fā shēng: hēi)
hook Nangun downward into hore stance chop
(shout: hey)

3.马步抛棍 mǎ bù pāo gùn
horse stance and rotate Nangun into block with ?
base upward

4.插步戳棍 chā bù chuō gùn
cross leg steps and thrust Nangun

5.高虚步滚压棍 gāo xū bù gǔn yā gùn
high empty stance and rotate Nangun into
downward press

6.马步戳棍 mǎ bù chuō gùn
horse stance with Nangun thrust

7.马步滚压棍 mǎ bù gǔn yā gùn
horse stance and rotate Nangun into downward press

8.独立步盖棍 dú lì bù gài gùn
stand on one leg and hit Nangun from top down

9.弓步拨棍(发声: 嗌) gōng bù bō gùn (fā shēng: yì)
bow stance with Nangun block

10.独立步背棍虎爪 dú lì bù bèi gùn hǔ zhǎo
stand on one leg and hold Nangun behind back
with tiger claw

11.背棍旋风腿 450° bèi gùn xuán fēng tuǐ 450°
tornade jump kick with Nangun behind back 450°

12.单蝶步背棍 dān dié bù bèi gùn
single butterfly step with Nangun behind back

13.高虚步击棍 gāo xū bù jī gùn
high empty stance and diagonally hit Nangun upward

14.马步挂劈棍 mǎ bù guà pī gùn
hook Nangun downward into horse stance chop

15.半马步截棍 bàn mǎ bù jié gùn
shifted horse stance and hit Nangun head forward

16.前跃半马步截棍 qián yuè bàn mǎ bù jié gùn
forward leap into shifted horse stance and hit
Nangun head forward

17.骑龙步击棍 qí lóng bù jī gùn
dragon-riding stance and diagonally hit
Nangun upward

18.腾空外摆腿 360° téng kōng wài bǎi tuǐ 360°
outisde jump kick 360°

19.马步挂劈棍（发声：嘿）
mǎ bù guà pī gùn (fā shēng: hēi)
hook Nangun downward into horse stance chop
(shout: hey)

第二段　　　　　　　　Part 2
20.骑龙步击把 qí lóng bù jī bǎ
dragon-riding stance and diagonally hit Nangun
base upward

21.上步左击棍 shàng bù zuǒ jī gùn
step forward and hit diagonally Nangun upward to left

22.上步右击把 shàng bù yòu jī bǎ
step forward and diagonally hit Nangun base
upward to right

23.上步左击棍 shàng bù zuǒ jī gùn
step forward and hit diagonally Nangun upward to left

24.上步圈压棍 shàng bù quān yā gùn
step forward and circle Nangun into press

25.盖步拨棍 gài bù bō gùn
cover step with Nangun block

26.蹬腿弹棍 dēng tuǐ dàn gùn
bend kick with heel and block Nangun downward

27.跳插步戳棍 tiào chā bù chuō gùn
jump into cross leg stance and thrust Nangun

28.跳插步戳把 tiào chā bù chuō bǎ
jump into cross leg stance and thrust Nangun base

29.单蝶步顶棍 dān dié bù dǐng gùn
single butterfly stance and hold Nangun head up
with base on ground

30.盖步绞棍 gài bù jiǎo gùn
cover step and circle Nangun base

31.弓步拨棍 gōng bù bō gùn
bow stance with Nangun block

32.马步挑劈棍 mǎ bù tiāo pī gùn
horse stance with flip Nangun head upward and
downward chop

33.弓步劈棍(发声: 嘿)
gōng bù pī gùn (fā shēng: hēi)
bow stance with Nangun chop (shout: hey)

34.马步挂劈棍 mǎ bù guà pī gùn
hook Nangun downward into horse stance chop

35.背棍旋风脚 360° bèi gùn xuán fēng jiǎo 360°
hold Nangun behind back and tornade jump kick 360°

36.单蝶步推棍 dān dié bù tuī gùn
single butterfly stance and push Nangun

37.腾空外摆腿 450° téng kōng wài bǎi tuǐ 450°
lotus jump kick 450°

38.马步背棍 mǎ bù bèi gùn
horse stance and hold Nangun behind back

39.高虚步击棍 gāo xū bù jī gùn
high empty stance and diagonally hit Nangun upward

40.独立步拨棍 dú lì bù bō gùn
stand on one leg with Nangun block

41.插步连环拨棍 chā bù lián huán bō gùn
cross leg steps with downward Nangun block
back and forth

42.马步崩棍 mǎ bù bēng gùn
horse stance and Nangun head flip upward

43.弓步拨棍 gōng bù bō gùn
bow stance with Nangun lower block

第三段   Part 3
44.弓步盖棍 gōng bù gài gùn
bow stance and hit Nangun from top down

45.弓步斜击棍 gōng bù xié jī gùn
bow stance and hit Nangun diagonally

46.马步挑把 mǎ bù tiāo bǎ
horse stance and flip Nangun base upward

47.骑龙步击棍 qí lóng bù jī gùn
dragon-riding stance and hit with Nangun

48.骑龙步击把 qí lóng bù jī bǎ
dragon-riding stance and hit with Nangun base

49.上步左右格棍 shàng bù zuǒ yòu gé gùn
step forward and block with Nangun vertically
on both sides

50.弓步弹棍 gōng bù dàn gùn
bow stance and block Nangun downward

51.跳插步抽棍 tiào chā bù chōu gùn
jump into cross leg stance and retract Nangun

52.腾空盘腿 360°侧扑 téng kōng pán tuǐ 360° cè pū
turning leg swing jump 360° into sideways laying

53.鲤鱼打挺 lǐ yú dǎ tǐng
kick up

54.单蝶步摔棍 dān dié bù shuāi gùn
single butterfly stance and slam Nangun

55.骑龙步架棍（发声：的）
qí lóng bù jià gùn (fā shēng : de)
dragon-ridign stance and upper block with Nangun
(shout: de)

56.独立步盖棍 dú lì bù gài gùn
stand on one leg and hit Nangun from top down

57.高虚步拨棍 gāo xū bù bō gùn
high empty stance and block Nangun downward

58.弓步挂劈棍 gōng bù guà pī gùn
hook Nangun downward into bow stance chop

第四段   Part 4
59.独立步拄棍 dú lì bù zhǔ gùn
stand on one leg and plant staff vertically on ground

60.左右舞花棍 zuǒ yòu wǔ huā gùn
circle block with Nangun on both sides

61.翻身跳单蝶步摔棍
fān shēn tiào dān dié bù shuāi gùn
turn and jump into single butterfly stance
and slam Nangun

62.弓步斜后挂棍 gōng bù xié hòu guà gùn
bow stance and hook Nangun diagonally backward

63.弓步劈棍 gōng bù pī gùn
bow stance with Nangun chop

64.弓步推棍（发声：嘿）
gōng bù tuī gùn (fā shēng : hēi)
bow stance and push Nangun (shout: hey)

65.虚步抽棍 xū bù chōu gùn
empty stance and retract Nangun

收势 shōu shì
closing form

A Group TaijiQuan (Tai Chi) Form
A组太极拳竞赛套路

预备势 yù bèi shì
preparation form

第一段　　　　　　**Part 1**

1.起势 qǐ shì
commencing form

2.揽雀尾 lǎn què wěi
grasp the peacock's tail

3.单鞭 dān biān
single whipo

4.白鹤亮翅 bái hè liàng chì
white crane spreads wings

5.搂膝拗步 lǒu xī ǎo bù
brush knee and twist steps on both sides

197

6.退步压肘 tuì bù yā zhǒu
step back and press elbows

7.腾空飞脚 téng kōng fēi jiǎ
front slap jump kick

8.腾空摆莲 360° téng kōng bǎi lián 360°
lotus kick 360°

9.雀地龙 què dì lóng
dragon dive to the ground

第二段　　　　　　　　Part 2
10.肘底捶 zhǒu dǐ chuí
fist under elbow

11.倒卷肱 dǎo juàn gōng
reverse reeling forearm, step back and repulse monkey
(left & right)

12.搬拦捶 bān lán chuí
turn body, deflect, parry, and punch

13.右蹬脚 yòu dēng jiǎo
kick with heel on right side

14.双峰贯耳 shuāng fēng guàn ěr
striking the opponent's ears with both fists

15.左分脚 zuǒ fēn jiǎo
Left toes kick

16.仆步下势 pū bù xià shì
move down into crouch stance

17.金鸡独立 jīn jī dú lì
golden rooster stands on one leg

18.旋风脚 180° xuán fēng jiǎo 180°
tornade jump kick 180°

19.独立托掌 dú lì tuō zhǎng
stand on one leg and raise palm

第三段   **Part 3**
20.指裆捶 zhǐ dāng chuí

21.野马分鬃 yě mǎ fēn zōng
part the wild horse's mane

22.海底针 hǎi dǐ zhēn
needle at sea bottom

23.闪通背 shǎn tōng bèi
horse stance with pull and choke

24.提手上势 tí shǒu shàng shì
raise hand above head

25.白鹤亮翅 bái hè liàng chì
white crane spreads its wings

26.后叉腿低势平衡 hòu chā tuǐ dī shì píng héng
low balance with leg crossed behind

第四段   **Part 4**
27.摆莲转体180° bǎi lián zhuǎn tǐ
lotus kick and turn body

28.独立抱掌 dú lì bào zhǎng
stand on one leg and hold palms

29.双震脚 shuāng zhèn jiǎo
stamping with both feet

30.蹬脚架推 dēng jiǎo jià tuī
heel kick with block and push

31.玉女穿梭 yù nǚ chuān suō
fair lady works with shuttles

32.云手 yún shǒu
wave hands like clouds

33.掩手肱捶 yǎn shǒu gōng chuí
hide hands and strike fist

34.揽雀尾 lǎn què wěi
grasp the peacock's tail

35.十字手 shí zì shǒu
cross hands

36.收势 shōu shì
closing form

A Group TaijiJian (Tai Chi Sword) Form
A组太极剑竞赛套路

预备势 yù bèi shì
preparation form

第一段   **Part 1**
1.起势 qǐ shì
commencing form

2.并步点剑(蜻蜓点水)
bìng bù diǎn jiàn (qīng tíng diǎn shuǐ)
stand with feet together and point sword
(dragonfly dip in the water)

3.弓步削剑(大鹏展翅)
gōng bù xiāo jiàn (dà péng zhǎn chì)
bow stance and cut obliquely
(great bird spreads its wings)

4.独立劈剑(力劈华山) dú lì pī jiàn (lì pī huá shān)
lift knee and chop sword
(vertically chop Huashan Mountain)

5.左弓步拦(迎风掸尘)
zuǒ gōng bù lán (yíng fēng dǎn chén)
left bow stance and parry sword
(dust in the direction of the wind)

6.左右撩剑(海底捞月)
zuǒ yòu liāo jiàn (hǎi dǐ lāo yuè)
circle upper sword block on left and right sides
(scooping up the moon from beneath the sea)

7.独立下刺(仙人指路)
dú lì xià cì (xiān rén zhǐ lù)
lift knee and thrust downward
(celestial being points the way)

8.退步回抽(盖拦穿心)
tuì bù huí chōu (gài lán chuān xīn)
step back and withdraw sword
(cover block and pierce through heart)

9.腾空飞脚 téng kōng fēi jiǎo
front slap jump kick

10.腾空摆莲360° téng kōng bǎi lián 360°
lotus jump kick 360°

11.雀地龙 què dì lóng
dragon dive to the ground

第二段   Part 2
12.弓步平刺(青龙出水)
gōng bù píng cì (qīng lóng chū shuǐ)
bow stance with horizontal thrust
(black dragon comes out of the water)

13.转身下刺(哪咤探海)
zhuǎn shēn xià cì (né zhā tàn hǎi)
turn body and thrust downward
(Nezha explores the sea)

14.弓步平斩(腰斩白蛇)
gōng bù píng zhǎn (yāo zhǎn bái shé)
bow stance and cut horizontally
(chop the middle of the white snake)

15.弓步崩剑(斜飞展翅)
gōng bù bēng jiàn(xié fēi zhǎn chì)
bow stance and flick sword (diagonally spread wings)

16.歇步压剑(风舞落叶) xiē bù yā jiàn (fēng wǔ luò yè)
rest stance and press sword
(fallen leaves dance in the wind)

17.进步绞剑(乌龙搅水)
jìn bù jiǎo jiàn (wū lóng jiǎo shuǐ)
step forward and twist the sword
(black dragon swirls the water)

18.独立上刺(宿鸟投林) dú lì shàng cì (sù niǎo tóu lín)
stand on one leg and stab up
(birds return to forests at nightfall)

19.虚步下截(乌龙摆尾) xū bù xià jié (wū lóng bǎi wěi)
empty stance and downward block
(black dragon shakes tail)

20.旋风脚180° xuán fēng jiǎo 180°
tornado jump kick 180°

21.独立上拖(独立挑帘)
dú lì shàng tuō (dú lì tiāo lián)
stand on one leg and hold up sword
(stand on one leg and lift the curtain)

第三段　　　　　　　　Part 3
22.进步挂剑(风动车轮)
jìn bù guà jiàn (fēng dòng chē lún)
advance and hook sword (wind blows the wheel)

23.虚步点剑(凤凰点头)
xū bù diǎn jiàn (fèng huáng diǎn tóu)
empty stance and point sword (phoenix nods its head)

24.蹬脚架剑(白云盖顶)
dēng jiǎo jià jiàn (bái yún gài dǐng)
heel kick and block with sword
(white cloud covers overhead)

25.后叉腿低势平衡 hòu chā tuǐ dī shì píng héng
low balance with leg crossed behind

26.摆莲转体180°独立 bǎi lián zhuǎn tǐ 180° dú lì
lotus kick and turn body 180° on one leg

27.歇步崩剑(古树盘根)
xiē bù bēng jiàn (gǔ shù pán gēn)
cross stance and tilt sword
(the old tree's roots overlap)

第四段　　　　　　　　Part 4
28.弓步下截(拨草寻蛇)
gōng bù xià jié (bō cǎo xún shé)
bow stance and intercept on both sides
(clear the grass to find the snake)

29.弓步下刺（哪吒探海）
gōng bù xià cì (nǎ zhà tàn hǎi)
bow stance and thrust sword (Nezha explores the sea)

30.右云抹剑（天马行空）
yòu yún mǒ jiàn (tiān mǎ xíng kōng)
right circle block overhead into slide with sword
(sky horse gallops above)

31.左云带剑（拨云望日）
zuǒ yún dài jiàn (bō yún wàng rì)
left circle block overhead into slide with sword
(brush away clouds to reveal the sun)

32.震脚下压（双震惊雷）
zhèn jiǎo xià yā (shuāng zhèn jīng léi)
stomp and press sword downward
(double stomp like thunder)

33.侧蹬下截（剑似离弦）
cè dēng xià jié (jiàn sì lí xián)
bend side kick and lower block with sword
(sword shoots fast like an arrow)

34.马步推剑（摘星换斗）
mǎ bù tuī jiàn (zhāi xīng huàn dǒu)
horse stance and push sword
(plucking the stars to change the constellations)

35.转身劈剑（蟒蛇翻身）
zhuǎn shēn pī jiàn(mǎng shé fān shēn)
turn around and chop sword (python flips over)

36.弓步上刺（饿虎扑食）
gōng bù shàng cì (è hǔ pū shí)
bow stance and thrust sword upward
(hungry tiger pounces on its prey)

37.仆步捧剑(叶底藏花)
pū bù pěng jiàn (yè dǐ cáng huā)
crouch stance and hold sword
(flowers hide under the leaves)

38.弓步直刺(金针指南)
gōng bù zhí cì (jīn zhēn zhǐ nán)
bow stance and thrust sword forward
(golden needle points south)

39.收势 shōu shì
closing form

A Group Taijishan (Tai Chi Fan) Form
A组太极扇竞赛套路

第一段   **Part 1**

1.起势 qǐ shì
opening form

2.震脚捧扇 zhèn jiǎo pěng shàn
take a stomp and hold the fan

3.横裆步持扇 héng dāng bù chí shàn
make a horizontal step with the fan

4.丁步插扇 dīng bù chā shàn
insert the fan in a t-step

5.丁步抛接扇 dīng bù pāo jiē shàn
throw the fan in a t-step

6.提膝穿扇 tí xī chuān shàn
raise the knee and slide the fan

7.弓步刺扇 gōng bù cì shàn
stab than fan and go into bowstance

8.虚步撩扇 xū bù liāo shàn
raise the fan in a circular motion and go
into empty stance

9.上步扫扇 shàng bù sǎo shàn
sweep the fan in an advancing step

10.提膝下刺扇 tí xī xià cì shàn
raise the knee and stab downward

11.退步抽扇 tuì bù chōu shàn
step back and draw the fan

12.腾空飞脚 téng kōng fēi jiǎo
jumping front slap kick

13.腾空摆莲360° téng kōng bǎi lián sān bǎi liù
jumping lotus kick 360°

14.跌叉开扇 diē chā kāi shàn
open the fan in the hurdler's position

第二段　　　　　　　Part 2
15.跟步开扇 gēn bù kāi shàn
make a follow-up step and open the fan

16.转身反持扇 zhuǎn shēn fǎn chí shàn
turn your body and hold the fan

17.歇步压扇 xiē bù yā shàn
press the fan downward in a resting stance

18.进步绞扇 jìn bù jiǎo shàn
step forward and twist the fan

19.跳弓步推扇 tiào gōng bù tuī shàn
bow stance jump and push with the fan

20.提膝上刺 tí xī shàng cì
raise the knee and stab upward

21.旋风脚180°开扇 xuàn fēng jiǎo yī bǎi bā kāi shàn
tornado kick 180° and open the fan

22.提膝抱扇 tí xī bào shàn
raise the knee and hold the fan

第三段   **Part 3**
23.左右挂扇 zuǒ yòu guà shàn
hook the fan on the left and right sides

24.虚步点扇 xū bù diǎn shàn
point the fan in an empty stance

25.蹬脚架扇 dēng jiǎo jià shàn
heel kick and block with fan

26.后插退低势平衡开扇
hòu chā tuì dī shì píng héng kāi shàn
low balance with leg crossed behind

27.提膝转体180°合扇 tí xī zhuǎn tǐ yī bǎi bā hé shàn
raise knee and turn 180° with fan closed

28.提膝独立 tí xī dúlì
single knee raise

29.弓步劈扇 gōng bù pī shàn
bow stance chop with fan

第四段　Part 4

30.云扇 yún shàn
cloud fan

31.翻身跳劈扇 fān shēn tiào pī shàn
turn and jump with a fan chop

32.提膝开扇 tí xī kāi shàn
raise knee and open the fan

33.马步肩靠 mǎ bù jiān kào
hit with shoulder in horse stance

34.震脚劈扇 zhèn jiǎo pī shàn
stomp and chop with fan

35.插步开扇 chā bù kāi shàn
open the fan with legs crossed

36.马步刺扇 mǎ bù cì shàn
stab with the fan in horse stance

37.跟步横击扇 gēn bù héng jī shàn
make a follow-up and step push with a horizontal fan

38.行步抹扇 xíng bù mǒ shàn
perform steps and a horizontal fan block

39.仆步捧扇 pū bù pěng shàn
bend down to crouch stance and hold the fan

40.收势 shōu shì
closing form

Regulations for Optional Routines (2019)
自选竞赛套路要求

Requirements for Optional Changquan, Jianshu, Daoshu, Qiangshu, and Gunshu
自选长拳、剑术，刀术、枪术、棍术套路的内容规定

Changquan shall contain at least three hand forms, namely, fist, palm and hook; three stances, namely, bow stance, horse-riding stance and empty stance; three leg techniques, namely, snap kick, sideward sole kick and back sweep; and elbow strike and cross-leg balance.

长拳至少包括拳、掌、勾三种手型；弓步、仆步、虚步三种主要步型；弹腿、踹腿、后扫腿三种腿法和顶肘及扣腿平衡。

Jianshu shall contain at least three main stances, namely, bow stance, horse-riding stance and empty stance; one longtime balance; and eight main apparatus-wielding methods, namely, thrust, upward parry, uppercut, point, chop, flick up, intercept, and figure 8 (necessarily including a complete set of upward parry from right and left followed by upward parry from the back).

剑术至少包括弓步、仆步、虚步三种主要步型；一个持久性平衡；刺剑、挂剑、撩剑、点剑、劈剑、截剑、崩剑、剪腕花等八种主要器械方法(其中必须有完整的左右挂剑接 背后穿挂剑)。

Daoshu shall contain at least three main stances, namely, bow stance, horse-riding stance and empty stance; eight main apparatus-wielding methods, namely, around-the-head twining, around-the-head wrapping, chop, thrust, hack, upward parry, cloud broadsword and back figure 8 (necessarily including a complete set of around-the-head twining and wrapping movements completed at a stretch).

刀术至少包括弓步、仆步、虚步三种主要步型；缠头、裹脑、劈刀、斩刀、挂刀、云刀、扎刀、背花刀等八种主要器械方法(其中必须有一次性完整的缠头裹脑刀)。

Qiangshu shall contain at least three main stances, namely, bow stance, horse-riding stance and empty stance; eight apparatus-wielding methods, namely, outward block, inward block, thrust, slide, tilt, point, figure 8 and end-tilt (necessarily including three consecutive sets of parry, catch and thrust completed at a stretch).

枪术至少包括弓步、仆步、虚步三种主要步型；拦枪、拿枪、扎枪、穿枪、崩枪、点枪、舞花枪、挑把等八种主要器械方法(其中必须有连续 3 个一次性完整的拦拿扎枪)。

Gunshu shall contain at least three main stances, namely, bow stance, horse-riding stance and empty stance; eight main apparatus-wielding methods, namely, downward strike, tilt, twist, horizontal swing, cloud cudgel, poke, figure 8, and uppercut carry (necessarily including three consecutive sets of carry, uppercut and figure 8 with both hands, to be completed at a stretch).

棍术至少包括弓步、仆步、虚步三种主要步型；劈棍、崩棍、绞棍、平抡棍、云棍、戳棍、舞花棍、提撩花棍等八种主要器械方法(其中必须有连续3个一次性完整的双手提撩花棍)。

Requirements for Optional Taijiquan and Taijijian
自选太极拳、太极剑套路的内容规定

Taijiquan shall contain at least two leg techniques; three main stances, namely, bow stance, horse-riding stance and empty stance; and eight main forms, namely, grasp the sparrow's tail, part the wild horse's mane, brush the knee, cloud hand, fair lady works at loom, cover hand and strike with arm , step back and curl arms, and deflect downward, parry and punch.

太极拳至少包括两种腿法；弓步、仆步、虚步三种主要步型；揽雀尾、野马分鬃、搂膝 国际武术套路竞赛规则 国际武术联合会 2005 年 11 月 12 拗步、云手、左右穿梭、掩手肱捶、倒卷肱、搬拦捶等八种主要动作。

Taijijian shall contain at least main three stances, namely, bow stance, crouch stance and empty stance; and eight main apparatus-wielding methods, namely, thrust, upward parry, uppercut, point, chop, intercept, slice and envelopment.

太极剑至少包括弓步、仆步、虚步三种主要步型；
刺剑、挂剑、撩剑、点剑、劈剑、截剑、抹剑、绞
剑等八种主要器械方法。

自选南拳、南刀、南棍套路的内容规定

Nanquan shall contain at least tiger's claw; two main
fist techniques, namely, downward strike with crossed
fist and uppercut; five stances, namely, bow stance,
crouch step, butterfly stance and dragon-riding stance;
and unicorn stance, side nail kick, and rolling bridge.

南拳至少包括虎爪；挂盖拳和抛拳两种主要拳法；
弓步、仆步、虚步、蝶步和骑龙步五种步型；以及
麒麟步、横钉腿和滚桥。

Nandao shall contain at least three main stances,
namely, bow stance, empty stance and dragon-riding
stance; eight main apparatus-wielding methods, namely, around-the-head twining, around-the-head wrapping, chop, slice, block, intercept, sweep, and figure 8
(necessarily including a complete set of around-the-
head twining and wrapping movements completed at a
stretch).

南刀至少包括弓步、虚步、骑龙步三种主要步型；
缠头、裹脑、劈刀、抹刀、格刀、截刀、扫刀、剪
腕花刀等八种主要器械方法(其中必须有一次性完整
的缠头裹脑刀)。

Nangun shall contain at least three main stances, namely, bow stance, empty stance and dragon-riding stance; and eight main apparatus-wielding methods, namely, downward strike, tilt, envelopment, roll together with cudgel, block, strike, top and throw.

南棍至少包括弓步、虚步、骑龙步三种主要步型；劈棍、崩棍、绞棍、滚压棍、格棍、击棍、顶棍、抛棍等八种主要器械方法。

Rank Testing Rules and Procedure
考级要求及申请程序

All qualified testers are required to complete the rank advancement application seven days before the testing date.
合格的申请者请在考试前7天提交考试申请表

Testers must check in with the testing officials at least 15 minutes before the scheduled time.
考试当天需至少提前15分钟到场检录

Any student who arrives after his/her scheduled testing time has started will be rescheduled for the following test.
考试时未到场的学员将安排下一次考试时间

A complete and clean school uniform (silk performance uniform is also acceptable); belt, and proper shoes are required to take the rank test.
考试时需着校训练服或丝质表演服装。

Test students are responsible for their own equipment and warm-up.

考试学员需准备好自己的器械并自己安排做好准备活动。

There is no exception to any of the above rules and procedures. Please note the calendar rank testing dates. Testing dates are subject to change as needed by discretion of Master Sitan Chen.

请学员遵守考试要求，并请注意日历上的考试日期。测试日期可能会根据主考老师的行程酌情更改。

Martial Arts （Wushu） Ranking Levels 少兒武術測試等級				
	Belt	**Basic Techniques**	**Routine**	**Level**
初级 Beginner	白 White	弓步，馬步，衝拳，亮掌，正踢，側踢，前拍脚 Bow Stance, Horse Stance, Punch, Palm, Straight Kick, Side Kick, Single Slap Kick	初级一段拳 Level 1 Fist	Beginner I
	白黃 White with Yellow Strip	白带的基本功+腾空弹踢，僕步，里合，外摆，单翻腰+坐盘 White belt Techniques + Jump Kick, Crouch Stance, Rotation Kick, Turn waist over + Cross-Legged Siting Stance	初级二段拳 Level 2 Fist	Beginner II
	黃 Yellow	白黄带的基本功+前扫，后扫，仆步穿掌，竖叉，大躍布前穿 White/Yellow belt Techniques + Forward Sweep, Backward Sweep, Crouch Stance pierce palm, Split, Forward giant leap	三路长拳 Primary Long Fist	Beginner III
	黃綠 Yellow with Green Stripe	黄带基本功+虚步，雙拍脚，弹腿，蹬腿，踹腿，腾空飞脚 Yellow belt Techniques + Empty Stance, Double Slap Kick, Forward Bent Kick, Side Bent Kick, Flying Front Kick	初级棍 Primary Staff Set	Beginner IV
	綠 Green	黄绿带基本功+旋风腿，腾空外摆莲 Yellow/ Green belt Techniques + Jumping Tornado kick, Flying Lotus Kick	初级剑/刀 Primary Sword/Broad Sword	Beginner V
中级 Intermediate	綠藍 Green(Blue Stripe)	绿带基本功+侧手翻+旋子 Green belt Techniques + Cartwheel+Butterfly Jump	Group B Chang Quan 1-2	Intermediate I
	藍 Blue	绿带基本功+侧手翻+旋子 Green belt Techniques + Cartwheel+Butterfly Jump	Group B Changquan 1-4	Intermediate II
	藍紅 Blue(Red Stripe)	蓝带基本功 + 跳躍组合 Blue belt Techniques + Jump Combinations	Group B Short Weapon	Intermediate III
	紅 Red	全套基本功 Whole Set of Basic Techniques	Group B Long Weapon	Intermediate IV
高级 Advanced	紅黑 Red(Black Stripe)	全套基本功，难度组合，自选套路 Whole Set of Basic Techniques, Difficulties, Optional Routines	Advance I
	黑 Black	全套基本功，难度组合，自选套路，太极 Whole Set of Basic Techniques, Optional Routines, Tai Chi	Advance II

Attached: Idiom-Based Martial Arts (Children's Version)
附: 成语武术操(少儿版)

Fundamental Wushu Movements for Young Beginners

1.一柱擎天挑重担 yī zhù qíng tiān tiāo zhòng dàn
  a pillar lifts the sky and carries the burden:
  Focusing on Holding the Fist with Steady Horse
  Stance

  - 并步抱拳 bìng bù bào quán
    feet together and hold fists

  - 右上冲拳左下按掌
    yòu shàng chōng quán zuǒ xià àn zhǎng
    upward punch with the right arm and downward
    press with the left palm

  - 左臂向上两拳头上交叉
    zuǒ bì xiàng shàng liǎng quán tóu shàng jiāo chā
    cross both wrists above the head

- 左跨步 zuǒ kuà bù
  left side step

- 马步双劈拳 mǎ bù shuāng pī quán
  horse stance with both fists striking down

- 收左脚并步抱拳 shōu zuǒ jiǎo bìng bù bào quán
  close the left foot and hold fists

- 右上冲拳左下按掌
  yòu shàng chōng quán zuǒ xià àn zhǎng
  upward punch with the right arm and downward
  press with the left palm

- 左臂向上两拳头上交叉
  zuǒ bì xiàng shàng liǎng quán tóu shàng jiāo chā
  cross both wrists above the head

- 右跨步 yòu kuà bù
  right side step

- 马步双劈拳 mǎ bù shuāng pī quán
  horse stance with both fists striking down

2.二龙戏珠更高招 èr lóng xì zhū gèng gāo zhāo
two dragons playing with a pearl:
Focusing on Sword Fingers, Single Leg Balance

- 并步抱拳 bìng bù bàoquán
  stand straight and hold fists

- 左抡臂剑指 zuǒ lūn bì jiàn zhǐ
  swirl the left arm while doing sword fingers

- 左开立甩头 zuǒ kāi lì shuǎi tóu
  left leg opens out and rotate the head

- 右提膝平衡 yòu tí xī pínghéng
  raise the right knee and balance

- 右落脚并步抱拳 yòu luò jiǎo bìng bù bào quán
  drop the right leg to close the feet and hold fists

- 右抡臂剑指 yòu lūn bì jiàn zhǐ
  swirl the right arm while doing sword fingers

- 右开立甩头 yòu kāi lì shuǎi tóu
  right leg opens out and rotate the head

- 左提膝平衡 zuǒ tí xī píng héng
  raise the left knee and balance

- 左落脚并步抱拳 zuǒ luò jiǎo bìng bù bào quán
  drop the left leg to close the feet and hold fists

3.三头六臂不寻常 sān tóu liù bì bù xún cháng
a hero with three heads and six arms (sea dragon
king's daughter): Focusing on Palms, Bow Stance

- 并步抱拳 bìng bù bào quán
  stand straight and hold fists

- 左弓步递时针双摆掌
  zuǒ gōng bù nì shí zhēn shuāng bǎi zhǎng
  left bow stance and swing both arms
  counterclockwise

- 右弓步顺时针双摆掌
  yòu gōng bù shùn shí zhēn shuāng bǎi zhǎng
  right bow stance and swing hands clockwise

- 马步双分掌 mǎ bù shuāng fēn zhǎng
  horse stance and push palms apart

- 马步合臂 mǎ bù hé bì
  horse stance and cross forearms

- 并步抱拳 bìng bù bào quán
  stand straight and hold fists

- 右弓步顺时针双摆掌
  yòu gōng bù shùn shí zhēn shuāng bǎi zhǎng
  right bow stance and swing right hand clockwise

- 左弓步顺时针双摆掌
  zuǒ gōng bù shùn shí zhēn shuāng bǎi zhǎng

- 马步双分掌 mǎ bù shuāng fēn zhǎng
  horse stance and push palms apart

- 马步合臂 mǎ bù hé bì
  horse stance and cross forearms

- 并步抱拳 bìng bù bào quán
  stand straight and hold fists

4.四平八稳推不倒，推不倒
sì píng bā wěn tuī bù dǎo, tuī bù dǎo
being steady and balanced with horse stance:
Focusing on Southern Style Palm with Horse Stance

- 并步抱拳 bìng bù bào quán
  stand straight and hold fists

- 马步抱拳 mǎ bù bào quán
  horse stance and hold fists

- 马步前推掌 mǎ bù qián tuī zhǎng
  horse stance and push with palms

- 马步双推指 mǎ bù shuāng tuī zhǐ
  horse stance and push with fingers

- 马步侧推指 mǎ bù cè tuī zhǐ
  horse stance and push to the sides with
  pushing fingers

- 马步抱拳 Mǎ bù bào quán
  horse stance and holding fists

- 并步直立 Bìng bù zhí lì
  bring feet together and stand straight

5. 五彩缤纷真神奇 wǔ cǎi bīn fēn zhēn shénqí
vibrancy and colors are spectacular:
Learning Small Combination Moves

- 并步抱拳 bìng bù bào quán
  stand straight and hold fists

- 左弓步抱拳顶肘右推掌
  zuǒ gōng bù bào quán dǐng zhǒu yòu tuī zhǎng
  left bow stance and hit with the elbow while the
  right hand pushes

- 绕臂跪步右抄拳 rào bì guì bù yòu chāo quán
  swing arms into kneeling stance and
  right hand uppercut

- 并步直立抱拳 bìng bù zhí lì bào quán
  stand straight and hold fists

- 右弓步抱拳顶肘左推掌 yòu gōng bù bào quán
  dǐng zhǒu zuǒ tuī zhǎng
  right bow stance and hit with the elbow while the
  left hand pushes

222

- 绕臂跪步左抄拳 rào bì guì bù zuǒ chāo quán
  swing arms into kneeling stance and left
  hand uppercut

- 并步抱拳 bìng bù bào quán
  stand straight and hold fists

6.六出祁山志不移 liù chū qí shān zhì bù yí
being very determined to accomplish the goal:
Focusing on Basic Attacking Movements

- 并步抱拳 bìng bù bào quán
  stand straight and hold fists

- 右虚步鞭拳按掌 yòu xū bù biān quán àn zhǎng
  right empty stance with a whip fist and
  pressing palm

- 右跪步抱拳左插掌
  yòu guì bù bào quán zuǒ chā zhǎng
  right kneeling stance and hold fists with
  left inserting palm

- 左转马步架掌 zuǒ zhuǎn mǎ bù jià zhǎng
  left turn into a horse stance with upper block palm

- 左弓步冲拳 zuǒ gōng bù chōng quán
  left bow stance punch

- 并步抱拳 bìng bù bào quán
  stand straight and hold fists

- 左虚步鞭拳按掌 zuǒ xū bù biān quán àn zhǎng
  left empty stance with a whip fist and
  pressing palm

223

- 左跪步抱拳左插掌
  zuǒ guì bù bào quán zuǒ chā zhǎng
  left kneeling stance and hold fists with left inserting palm

- 右转马步架掌 zuǒ zhuǎn mǎ bù jià zhǎng
  right turn into a horse stance with upper block palm

- 右弓步冲拳 yòu gōng bù chōng quán
  right bow stance punch

- 并步抱拳 bìng bù bào quán
  stand straight and hold fists

7.七十二变人难料 qī shí èr biàn rén nán liào
Monkey King can transform into seventy-two beings: Introducing T-step Move into Single Leg Balance

- 并步抱拳 bìng bù bào quán
  stand straight and hold fists

- 左丁步双勾手 zuǒ dīng bù shuāng gōu shǒu
  left T-step and hook both arms

- 左提膝勾手反掌 zuǒ tí xī gōu shǒu fǎn zhǎng
  raise left knee, hook hand, and turn the palm over

- 左落脚并步抱拳 zuǒ luò jiǎo bìng bù bào quán
  drop the right leg to close the feet and hold fists

- 右丁步双勾手 yòu dīng bù shuāng gōu shǒu
  right T-step and hook both hands

- 右提膝勾手反掌 yòu tí xī gōu shǒu fǎn zhǎng
  raise right knee, hook hand, and turn the palm over

- 右落脚并步抱拳 yòu luò jiǎo bìng bù bào quán
  drop the right leg to close the feet and hold fists

8.八仙过海显神通 bā xiān guò hǎi xiǎn shén tōng
eight immortals cross the sea and show their magical
powers:Introducing Southern Style Fist Swing

- 并步抱拳 bìng bù bào quán
  stand straight and hold fists

- 左弓步抛拳 zuǒ gōng bù pāo quán
  left bow stance and swing arms

- 右弓步抛拳 yòu gōng bù pāo quán
  right bow stance and swing arms

- 马步按掌 mǎ bù àn zhǎng
  horse stance and press palm

- 右弓步上冲拳 yòu gōng bù shàng chōng quán
  right bow stance and punch upward

- 并步抱拳 bìng bù bào quán
  stand straight and hold fists

- 右弓步抛拳 yòu gōng bù pāo quán
  right bow stance and swing arms

- 左弓步抛拳 zuǒ gōng bù pāo quán
  left bow stance and swing arms

- 马步按掌 mǎ bù àn zhǎng
  horse stance and press palm

- 左弓步上冲拳 zuǒ gōng bù shàng chōng quán
  left bow stance and punch upward

225

9.九九归一繁做简 jiǔ jiǔ guī yī fán zuò jiǎn)
making difficult and complicated things simple:
Learning Southern Style push Palms

- 并步抱拳 bìng bù bàoquán
  stand straight and hold fists

- 马步叠掌 mǎ bù dié zhǎng
  horse stance with stacking palms

- 左弓步推掌 zuǒ gōng bù tuī zhǎng
  left bowstance and push palms

- 马步叠掌 mǎ bù dié zhǎng
  horse stance with stacking palms

- 右弓步推掌 yòu gōng bù tuī zhǎng
  right bow stance and push palms

- 并步抱拳 bìng bù bào quán
  stand straight and hold fists

- 马步叠掌 mǎ bù dié zhǎng
  horse stance with stacking palms

- 右弓步推掌 yòu gōng bù tuī zhǎng
  right bow stance and push palms

- 马步叠掌 mǎ bù dié zhǎng
  horse stance with stacking palms

- 左弓步推掌 zuǒ gōng bù tuī zhǎng
  left bowstance and push palms

- 并步抱拳 bìng bù bào quán
  stand straight and hold fists

10.十拿九稳乐陶陶 shí ná jiǔ wěn lè táo táo
happiness from being confident about success:
Learning Northern Style Palms Movements

- 并步抱拳 bìng bù bàoquán
  stand straight and hold fists

- 左弓步右砍掌 zuǒ gōng bù yòu kǎn zhǎng
  left bow stance and chop with right palm

- 右弓步左砍掌 yòu gōng bù zuǒ kǎn zhǎng
  right bowstance and chop with left palm

- 马步收掌 mǎ bù shōu zhǎng
  horse stance and bring palms in

- 独立侧推掌 dú lì cè tuī zhǎng
  balance on one leg and push palms

- 并步抱拳 bìng bù bào quán
  stand straight and hold fists

- 右弓步左砍掌 yòu gōng bù zuǒ kǎn zhǎng
  right bowstance and chop with left palm

- 左弓步右砍掌 zuǒ gōng bù yòu kǎn zhǎng
  left bow stance and chop with right palm

- 马步收掌 mǎ bù shōu zhǎng
  horse stance and bring palms in

- 独立侧推掌 dú lì cè tuī zhǎng
  balance on one leg and push palms